Coronado's Land

Essays on Daily Life in Colonial New Mexico

⊕

Marc Simmons

University of New Mexico Press
Albuquerque

Library of Congress Cataloging-in-Publication Data

Simmons, Marc.
    Coronado's land: essays on daily life in colonial New Mexico/
Marc Simmons. — 1st ed.
        p. cm.
    Includes bibliographical references (p.   ) and index.
    ISBN 0-8263-1313-2   0-8263-1702 (pbk)
        1. Spaniards—New Mexico—Social life and customs—
Anecdotes. 2. New Mexico—Social life and customs—
Anecdotes. I. Title
    F799.S59 1991
    978.9'00461—dc20 ˙   91-21689
                                                          CIP

Permission is acknowledged for the right to reproduce the
following essays by Marc Simmons:

    El Palacio, Quarterly Magazine of the Museum of New
    Mexico, Spring 1983 (V. 89 No. 1): "New Mexico's Colonial
    Agriculture."

    The Spanish Colonial Arts Society, Inc., Hispanic Arts and
    Ethnohistory in the Southwest: New Papers Inspired by the Work of
    E. Boyd, edited by Marta Weigle (Santa Fe: Ancient City Press,
    1983): "Carros y Carretas: Vehicular Traffic on the Camino
    Real."

    Southwest Heritage, Winter 1982–1983 (V. 12 No 4): "New
    Mexican Ciboleros on the Buffalo Plains."

    Historical Society of New Mexico. "Account of Disorders in
    New Mexico, 1778."

    New Mexico Historical Review, 1985 (V. 60 No. 1): "The Chacón
    Economic Report of 1803."

For
the Paloheimos
of
el Rancho de las Golondrinas

Contents

PART TWO

Preface

I n his charming little book, *The Land of Poco Tiempo*,
author Charles F. Lummis declared a century ago that
colonial New Mexico had witnessed some of the most
incredible pioneering the world has ever seen. The early
Spanish settlers, he concluded from his archival re-
searches and tale-collecting, had made superhuman
marches, suffered awful privations, and shown the most
devoted heroism. Lummis, who tended to view the past
through a romantic lens, was prone to exaggeration, but
his enthusiasm for things Hispanic and subjects New
Mexican was altogether genuine.

I borrowed some of that enthusiasm when long ago
I eagerly read *The Land of Poco Tiempo* and other Lummis
titles on the Southwest. He was an outsider, just as I
was, who approached the land and people of New Mexico from afar and had become captivated by their rich

story. Outsiders can never quite capture and explain the essence of a culture, which is properly the task of a native insider. But they can bring to bear a detached perspective that is useful in gaining a broad understanding of one society's nature and history.

In 1958 I enrolled in Professor France V. Scholes's graduate history class, the Hispanic Southwest, at the University of New Mexico. Scholes, then near retirement, was a leading colonialist scholar. From him I acquired a more serious and in-depth view of the subject than had been available in my earlier readings of Lummis. In fact, the Scholes course cemented my resolve to make the Spanish heritage of New Mexico a focus of my own future research, writing, teaching, and public lecturing. One result of that life-long commitment is the present book.

Over the years, delving deeper into the field, I developed a fascination for everyday things—domestic life, traditional customs, material culture—that other historians often overlook or ignore. Knowing how people from the past made a living, what tools and household articles they used, and how they behaved toward one another can sometimes be as important as following the themes of politics, war, and international relations. In Part One I have selected twenty of my shorter essays that in various ways illuminate daily life among old-time Hispanic New Mexicans. My aim here is to open a small window on their social history, but one that the general reader will find interesting and worthy of attention.

In Part Two I have included three translated documents from the later colonial period and to each have added a short introduction. All three are loaded with the kinds of small details that prove useful in reconstructing ways of life that have long since vanished. Historians refer to such documents as primary sources since they provide the basic information that allows us to learn what happened in the past and then interpret it.

New Mexico in its colonial era went through various stages of exploration and colonization. Francisco Vásquez de Coronado opened the story with his spectacular expedition of discovery in the years 1540 to 1542. Another cavalier, Don Juan de Oñate, initiated settlement in 1598 and twelve years later the capital of Santa Fe had its beginnings. The civilian colony lagged behind for the next seven decades as the Franciscan missions, dedicated to conversion of the Pueblo Indians, flourished. The entire Spanish enterprise, however, collapsed in 1680 when the oppressed Pueblos united in a massive revolt.

After Don Diego de Vargas reasserted Spain's rule in 1692, returning settlers launched a new period of colonization. Having been humbled by their earlier defeat, they worked to create an atmosphere of harmony between themselves and the Pueblos. As a result, New Mexicans of the eighteenth century displayed a steadiness, a willingness to endure, and an adaptability not evident among their predecessors of the prerevolt years.

By the final quarter of the colonial era, that is, the last years of the eighteenth and first two decades of the nineteenth centuries, a unique New Mexican way of life had crystalized in the watershed of the upper Rio Grande. A distinctive geography, the influence of surrounding Indian peoples, and the normal developmental process of communities in isolation all combined to produce this new regional style or tradition. It was one that would persist past Mexican Independence, through the time of Anglo-American penetration in the latter nineteenth century, and would survive in varying degrees to the present day.

Against that background, the essays collected in this book, most of them published originally elsewhere, can be fitted. If one seeks an underlying theme, I believe it can be found in the Hispanic New Mexicans's ongoing struggle to come to terms with their beautiful but grudging homeland and in their efforts to adapt and make do with what the frontier had to offer. Their story, even in its smallest details, deserves not to be forgotten.

Marc Simmons
Cerrillos, NM
March 1991

Part One

When New Mexicans
Dressed in Skins

I n 1598 Don Juan de Oñate and a wagon train of colonists marched north from the El Paso Valley to establish the first Spanish settlement in the Southwest.
They expected to prosper and to create a shining center
of Hispanic civilization on the upper Rio Grande.

With that in mind the first settlers brought with
them the fancy clothes they had been accustomed to
wearing in central Mexico. The men had splendid velvet
suits with high fluted collars and lace cuffs. They also
wore sateen caps and expensive shoes from Cordova,
Spain, richly carved and stitched. The women in the
cavalcade were no less gaudily attired. Many had full
silk dresses decorated with gold piping and lacy trim.
Their hair was held by tortoise shell combs and covered
with expensive fringed and embroidered shawls im-

ported from Manila. They were shod in dainty slippers of bright colors.

As it turned out, New Mexico proved to be so poor that no one was able to build palaces and mansions, for which such clothing might have been appropriate. Velvet and silk served well in the great cities farther south. But on the frontier they were totally impractical. Before long the colonists packed away their finery and took to dressing like the Indians. In other words, they began wearing clothes made of gamuza. That was simply buckskin, the softly tanned hide of deer and antelope, which abounded in the province.

So far as I am aware, no one has ever made a study of the use of gamuza by the Spanish settlers. It was not only a popular material for clothing, but it had many other functions. We have just about forgotten, I suspect, that gamuza was once an integral part of daily life in New Mexico.

The change over from costly cloth to inexpensive buckskin began at an early date. In 1602 Juan de Montoya, one of the Oñate colonists, wrote that most people wore chamois, or buckskin, because it offered more warmth in the winter. That was true, except when wet; then it was uncomfortably cold and clammy.

The Pueblo Indians were superb hunters and had stacks of skins in the village storerooms. At first the Spaniards acquired these by trade. But later they took up hunting and obtained hides to produce their own gamuza. They also probably got some of their tanning methods from the Indians, although the basic process was familiar to them. To start, several rawhides with the flesh removed were placed in a wooden trough. I have also seen a large outdoor pit lined with rocks that

From cap to shoes, the eighteenth-century New Mexican at right is dressed in tanned buckskin and leather. The aristocrat on horseback wears leather *botas* and coat. (From a drawing by Jose Cisneros)

was said to have been used as a tanning vat in colonial days.

To the container, water was added along with the root of *caña agria*. This plant, a member of the buckwheat family, was gathered in the mountains of New Mexico. The roots resemble the sweet potato and contain large amounts of tannin, an acid needed to prepare buckskin. After the hides soaked for two weeks in the water and caña agria, they were removed, wrung out, and the hair was scraped off. For the scraping, the wet hide was draped over a sloping log in the yard and a curved blade, called a beam knife, was used to remove the hair. Afterward, boiled brains were rubbed into the hide to render it supple and soft.

Most buckskins were left a pleasing natural color. But some were bleached white in the tanning process and others were colored by smoking or by use of paint. The finished product was much in demand in the mining communities of northern Mexico where cheap clothing was always needed for the workers. Carts by the hundreds, loaded with gamuza, must have rumbled southward on the old Spanish trail during the colonial period. Indeed, buckskin was considered so valuable that single pieces served as a medium of exchange. Other, less common items were said to be worth so many gamuzas.

Some of the finest buckskin was set aside to be used as artists' canvas. On it were painted images of the saints or other religious scenes. In a few of New Mexico's oldest churches it is still possible to see examples of these skin paintings. They represent some of the earliest folk art to be found in the Southwest.

The poorest grade of buckskin was reserved for the

making of a wide assortment of useful items. These included tobacco pouches, letter holders, and water bags. Large skin sacks were filled with grain for transport by burros.

When the Santa Fe Trail was opened in 1821, great quantities of cheap American cloth began to enter the New Mexican market. But many years elapsed before it managed to completely displace the homemade gamuza. In the 1850s merchant William Napton visited a large adobe house on the edge of the plains near Las Vegas. He described it as, "an extensive buckskin tailoring establishment where they were manufacturing clothes of various patterns. I was surprised at the skill in making the garments. The clothes were made to fit with tailor-like precision and exactness. Buckskin was generally worn at that time by the inhabitants of New Mexico."

What Napton saw was the tag end of a long tradition. For within a few years the railroad arrived bringing economical cloth from the mills of New England. Gamuza could not compete. By the opening of the twentieth century, it had all but disappeared, except among the Pueblo Indians who continued to use it for some of their ceremonial costumes.

Today if you want a piece of hand tanned gamuza, you will have to get it from them. But now it fetches a premium price!

On the Trail
of the Footless Stockings

⚜

In recent years I have gained a reputation, among some historians and anthropologists, as the only expert on Spanish footless stockings. I appear to have won that dubious title because no one else seems interested in them.

My expertise, if such it is, was acquired more by accident than design. From a long study of the history of colonial New Mexico, I had learned that one of the chief products of local manufacture in the seventeenth and eighteenth centuries was wool stockings. Several of the more unscrupulous Spanish governors operated illegal sweatshops in the adobe palace at Santa Fe. They would force Indian women to work long hours with little or no pay, weaving blankets and knitting stockings. Once a year, they would bundle up these articles and ship them down to El Paso and beyond for sale. The governors pocketed all the profits.

Often, I wondered what those stockings might have looked like. Being highly perishable, no examples are known to survive from the colonial period.

Then one day I happened to be reading the colonial chronicle of a German Jesuit priest with the improbable name of Ignaz Pfefferkorn. Father Pfefferkorn had come to Sonora (the Mexican province southwest of New Mexico) as a missionary to the Indians in the 1760s. While there he had written a lengthy description of life and customs, which a few years ago was translated into English and published.

Quite by chance I ran onto a reference to stockings in the priest's account. How strange are the people of Sonora, he remarked, for they wear stockings from New Mexico that have no feet.

There was my first clue to the appearance of these garments—NO FEET! Since Father Pfefferkorn expressed such surprise, that suggested he hadn't seen similar footgear anywhere else in Mexico. Was it possible that footless socks were made only in New Mexico, and if so, why?

Not long afterward I was visiting an open-air market at one of the Indian pueblos on the Rio Grande. At the stall of an old blanket-wrapped woman, I suddenly spied a pair of new-made, black wool stockings without any feet. There they were: a perfect example of the same article that must have been made here in colonial times. Now I knew exactly how they looked.

These stockings resemble what are today called "tube socks," manufactured without feet and sold in sporting goods stores. Indians, who still use their own knitted

An Isleta Pueblo woman, winnowing on the threshing floor, wears
traditional footless stockings. (Arizona State Museum)

variety, pull the ends under their heels so that the upper half of the foot is covered and the toes are left bare. A little investigation turned up the fact that a number of elderly Pueblos and Navajos continue to wear these traditional stockings.

Recently, I've discovered in museums several *santos*, wooden saints carved in colonial New Mexico, whose toes are sticking out from the end of open black stockings. Since the saintmakers usually clothed the figures in the everyday dress of their own period, this evidence would seem to prove that the early Spaniards wore the same kind of stockings made by the Indians today.

One important question remains. Why did the New Mexicans of long ago—both Spanish and Indian—take up the impractical custom of using stockings without feet? That's something I still haven't figured out.

Frontier Hairdressing

⚜

I t appears that from the beginning of recorded history, men and women have paid considerable attention to personal grooming. Almost everyone is born with a streak of vanity and wants to look their best when appearing in public. Many peoples of the world paint their faces, and some go so far as to decorate forehead, cheek, and chin with elaborate tattoos.

Hair styles have always played a major role in good grooming. Today, hair fashions are apt to change from year to year, in contrast to times past when one style came in vogue and remained popular from one century to another.

The Indians and Spaniards inhabiting the upper Rio Grande Valley in colonial days had a distinctive way of dressing their locks, one that conformed to ancient custom and perfectly suited them.

12

The first requirement for both men and women was that the hair be left long. Males formed their heavy manes in two braids that hung down the back, sometimes as far as the waist. Every man took special pride in his hair. The braids showed that he was a good and honorable citizen, and he would fight to preserve them.

Short hair was a mark of dishonor. Only criminals, those recently released from jail, went about with their heads close-cropped. Such a man was called *El Pelón*, or "Baldy." He was a social outcast and decent people refused to associate with him.

Women wore a single braid, knotted and tied up on the back of their heads. It was a symbol of virtue. Ladies guilty of some moral indiscretion might be seized by their fellow villagers and, with the snip of the scissors, shorn of their precious hair. No punishment was more severe, for the victim faced taunts and scorn from the community while the hair grew back. Until that happened, she was addressed only as "La Pelona."

The Pueblo Indians took as much pride in their long hair as the Spaniards. It even assumed some religious significance, since during dances and ceremonies the hair was unbraided and allowed to fall freely down the back.

In the earliest days, Spanish provincial officials and missionaries were in the habit of chopping off Indian locks as punishment for the slightest misconduct. The practice proved demoralizing to the natives. Humiliated, they ran off to the mountains to hide, and some even committed suicide. When the viceroy in Mexico City learned of this, he sent an order to New Mexico's governor in 1620 prohibiting such brutal barberings. These haircuts, he noted, were causing the Indians to abandon

13

A hair style once popular among Indian and Hispanic women. (From W. H. Emory, *Notes of a Military Reconnoissance* [1848])

what little Christianity they had taken up and to become bitter enemies of the Spaniards.

Besides the use of braids, the Pueblos had another hair style still occasionally seen today. It was formed by tying the hair in a double loop and wrapping it with a white or colored sash (called a *faja* by the Spaniards) to make a thick "club" at the back of the head. Known as a *chongo*, the club style remains most popular now among the Navajo, both men and women wearing it.

One serious problem in having long hair on the New Mexico frontier was that it invariably got infested with lice. Bugs on the head was something people got accustomed to and did their best to combat.

The only proven method for delousing was to do the job by hand. Husband and wife customarily performed the service for each other. Sometimes several ladies would get together for an afternoon's "delousing party." Chatting merrily, they would go over one another's scalps picking out the lice and crushing them between the fingers, or occasionally the teeth. If a man looked in on the party, all activity came to an embarrassed halt. It was not considered proper for a woman to be seen actually engaged in such a chore.

In a curious way, the lice problem helped bring about a change in the hair style of New Mexican men. When the first Americans reached the Rio Grande in the 1820s, the native people were astonished to see that, although they were not criminals, they went around with short hair. In time, this custom of grooming introduced by the newcomers helped break down the old prejudice against people with close-trimmed locks. But a major blow against the custom of long braids was not struck until 1864.

In that year, Kit Carson led a major expedition against the hostile Navajo living in the arid deserts of western New Mexico. His force consisted of regular army troops and companies of volunteer native militia drawn from Hispanic towns up and down the Rio Grande. The campaign was long and difficult. Water was scarce and little time existed for personal "clean-ups." The militiamen became infested with lice. They could not sleep for the itching and scratched their heads until many broke out in sores. Morale sunk to a low ebb, and the fighting efficiency of the companies waned.

Finally, their own officers took a hand and issued a stern order. Everyone must be clipped; the braids had to go. Some men wept and begged to be allowed to keep their hair. They didn't relish being called *pelones* when they returned home.

But the order stood and with the clip-clip of the shears, black strands fell in heaps to the ground. Only a few old men, who proclaimed they were ready to die first, were spared. When the volunteer soldiers reached home, minus their beloved braids, the ridicule they had expected was nowhere in evidence. Since so many young men were in the same boat, the young ladies were not about to raise a storm against them.

That single incident cracked the iron bands of custom, and thereafter, the traditional hair braids for men went rapidly out of fashion.

How Colonial Ladies
Painted Their Faces

⟡

S ince ancient times people have tried to improve their personal appearance by the use of cosmetics. Egypt's Cleopatra and her ladies-in-waiting applied green eyeshadow made of copper sulfate. In Rome Emperor Nero and his wife daubed their cheeks with white lead and chalk to lighten the skin. Mary, Queen of Scots, took wine baths to beautify her complexion.

From the simple and inexpensive preparations of antiquity, the use of cosmetics has ballooned today into a multi-million dollar industry. Now the emphasis is as much on hiding age as highlighting beauty.

On the New Mexico frontier of a century ago, Spanish women developed their own aids for facial improvement, using locally available mineral and vegetable products. They applied cosmetics so heavily that many of the first Anglos entering the territory were shocked.

These men came from prim eastern society where proper women did not rouge or powder their faces.

The universal cosmetic of the Southwest was flour-paste, plastered in a thick coat from forehead to chin. It gave the appearance of a mask and one purpose was to protect the skin from the sun. A Yankee lawyer upon first observing ladies wearing a covering of flour wrote: "They remain in this repulsive condition two or three weeks upon the eve of a grand ball or fiesta at which they desire to appear in all their freshness and beauty."

Powdered chalk was sometimes substituted for flour. To both, women generally added some form of red coloring. German traveler Baldwin Mollhausen, visiting the Rio Grande Valley in the 1850s, spoke of the use of blood. "Faces of the feminine sex peeped curiously as we passed by the farms," he recorded. "But neither age, nor youth, beauty, nor ugliness could be discerned through the mask of chalk or the blood of cattle, with which they had seen fit to bedaub themselves."

More commonly used as a rouge than cow's blood was a plant called *alegría,* which was red cockscomb. Maidens crushed the flowers, spit on them, then rubbed the crimson coloring on their cheeks.

George Ruxton, a somewhat snobbish British youth, toured Mexico in 1846. Passing through Chihuahua and El Paso, he reached Socorro where he found that "the women besmear themselves with fresh coats of *alegría* when their faces become dirty; thus their countenances are covered with alternate strata of paint and dirt, caked and cracked in fissures."

The heavy layers of powder and red paint served a function the critics never seemed to notice. They helped disguise pock marks, the terrible scars left by smallpox,

Vicenta Labadie de Chaves was famous for her delicate beauty in the nineteenth century. (From the collection of Marc Simmons)

with which practically all New Mexicans in the old days were afflicted. If the Spanish ladies applied it a little too thickly to suit Anglo tastes, they had a reason. And, of course, some Hispanic women needed little makeup for their natural beauty to be obvious.

Actually in some conservative New Mexican families, over-use of cosmetics was frowned upon. If a girl applied too heavy a coat of powder, one of her elders at the dinner table might say casually, "¡A esta se le volco la olla!" meaning, "This young lady seems to have let the pot boil over." The remark referred to the ash cloud that rose and covered the cook's face when she allowed a boiling pot to spill in the fire. Thus shamed, the girl would rush from the table and scrub off the powder.

An Unmentionable Subject

✥

C hamber pots and privies! Were they used by the early Spaniards in the Southwest? That is a question that nearly all historians and writers have chosen to ignore. In fact, the Spanish colonists themselves in their records almost never mentioned the topic of human waste disposal.

It is, nevertheless, one of the chief factors affecting personal hygiene, for careless handling of waste can spread a variety of diseases. For centuries, Europeans were in the habit of throwing the contents of chamber pots and kitchen slops out the window, so that their streets were open sewers. Passers-by had to dodge lively to keep from being hit.

Larger cities on the continent had public latrines, some of them extending over rivers and streams, which carried away the waste. Others were built upon cesspits, with the ordure periodically removed and taken to fertilize surrounding fields. In Spanish municipalities, toilet facilities were reported to be of the most primitive kind, there being no public sanitary arrangements. As a result the conquistadors, upon arriving in the New World, were astonished by the cleanliness of the Indian towns as compared to their own.

As an example, we can take note of a remark by Pedro de Castañeda, chronicler of the Coronado expedition. While in New Mexico, he observed that: "The [Pueblo] villages are free of nuisances because they go outside to excrete, and they pass their water into clay vessels, which they empty at a distance from the village."

Three and a half centuries later, in 1880, archeologist-historian Adolph F. Bandelier found the Indian practice still intact. At Santo Domingo Pueblo, for instance, he noted: "On every roof there was the *tinaja* (jar) with the urine of the night, which smelt ugly. They carry it out into the fields." Among other things, his statement seems to confirm that the Pueblos recognized the value of human waste as a fertilizing agent.

And they had another use for the contents of their tinajas. Urine is a weak acid that can be mixed with indigo and other coloring to fix the dye to yarn. Like the Indians, Hispanic New Mexicans also employed urine as a mordant. Not until the Anglos introduced artificial dyes after 1850 was the practice abandoned along the upper Rio Grande.

To what degree did the colonial settlers imitate the Pueblo Indians in their careful removal of waste? We cannot be certain simply because its mention occurs only rarely in the Spanish documents. The Franciscan missionaries usually had latrines within their *conventos* (living quarters) attached to the church, but those in-house sanitary facilties are about the only ones ever noted.

At the mission of Tajique Pueblo in 1663, toilets existed in the convento and were used by the Indians as well as the friars. At Picuris Pueblo in 1747, the convento had, says a contemporary report, "an upper room for privies, roofed, with its two-seat box." But at Acoma, the latrine was located in a corner of the convento's open courtyard and was described in 1776 by Father Francisco Domínguez as "a small recess for certain necessary business."

How these facilities were maintained and their contents regularly emptied is left unrecorded. Possibly, as was done elsewhere, the friars dumped wood ashes in the privy holes to serve as a chemical reagent. They also may have furnished the latrines with corncobs, for use in place of toilet paper, as was the custom in some parts of New Spain.

At present there is little to indicate the existence in New Mexico of free-standing privies or in-house chambers functioning as latrines much before the late nineteenth century, at least in the traditional domestic setting. Some Indian pueblos did not adopt the "whiteman's privy" until after World War I.

Rural New Mexicans probably were accustomed to relieve themselves in the great outdoors. But like their urban neighbors, they must have owned a chamber pot (*bacín*) for use inside during cold weather. The accepted procedure was to dispose of waste from chamber pots on the nearest farmland, as the Indians did with their tinajas.

No one has chosen to specialize in the study of

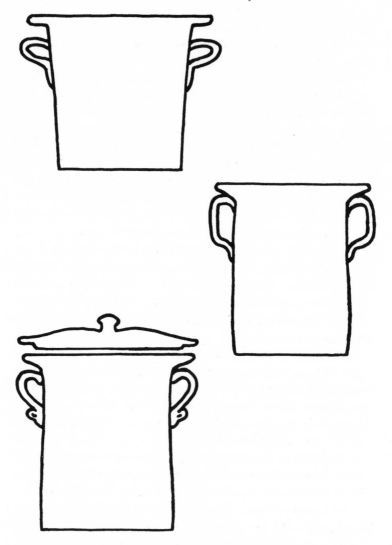

Some basic forms of Hispanic chamber pots. (Courtesy Archeological Society of New Mexico)

Spanish chamber pots, so our knowledge of these vessels is somewhat sketchy. Wills and inventories from the colonial era refer to pots of silver, copper, porcelain, and common clay. The wealthy classes in Mexico City occasionally obtained handsome ceramic chamber pots manufactured in Sevilla, and a few of those found their way north, possibly, to the New Mexico frontier.

One wonders how in open country, travelers with the great caravans plying the Camino Real managed to preserve their modesty when nature called. The practice of later American pioneers was learned by historian Dale L. Morgan from a Mormon lady whose grandmother went to Utah by ox train.

According to what the grandmother had told her many years ago, "When the trains set out, the captain immediately established this rule: women to go to this side, men to that. And on the flat and treeless plains, Mormon women solved the problem of privacy by walking out in a group, several standing with skirts spread wide to provide a screen for their sisters."

That, concludes Dr. Morgan, must have been the system employed in all family wagon trains going West. In all likelihood, some similar arrangement must have been adopted by the huge caravans that moved in and out of New Mexico for centuries. But we may never know the precise details since the matter was considered too indelicate by contemporaries to write about.

Of Ink and Pens

W hat did the early-day Spaniards in the Southwest do for writing ink?" someone asked me recently.

"Did they make their own ink here," he wanted to know, "or did they bring it from Mexico, or maybe even Spain?" These are questions, I believe, that no one has ever tried to answer.

In all my searching through colonial documents, I've never found a reference to the Spaniards importing ink to New Mexico. But, I feel sure in fact they did.

This is suggested by the writing seen in many of the books of baptisms, marriages, and deaths preserved in the archives of the Catholic Church. The Spanish padres began their entries with a script that is still dark and plain. But as you turn the pages, it becomes weak and faded.

What happened apparently was this: when a wagon

train from Mexico arrived with supplies, ink was distributed to the missions. For a time it remained plentiful, the padres making nice entries in their record books. But since there were long intervals between caravans, the ink supply dwindled. To stretch it, the fathers added more and more water, until finally the color was so weak it could, in some cases, hardly be read.

The imported or "commercial" ink would have been made from a formula common then in Spain and other parts of Europe. In a water solution, tannic acid obtained from the bark of trees was mixed with iron oxide. This produced a black ink. But owing to the oxide, as the script faded over the centuries it turned a reddish brown. That's the color on most of the Spanish documents kept today in the State Archives at Santa Fe.

If some ink was originally brought to New Mexico by ox cart, it must have been terribly expensive. Probably too costly for most people outside the government or Church. And, as a matter of fact, we know that the local people were accustomed to get along with homemade ink.

There were probably several recipes for ink, all of them simple. Archeologist Adolph Bandelier tells of one he collected among the Indians of Cochiti Pueblo north of Albuquerque in the 1880s. They wrote on sheepskin and he says: "The ink they made of pulverized charcoal, mixed with water, saliva or 'slime' to bind it." Since the Indians had learned writing from the Spaniards, they must have borrowed this ink formula, too.

Another recipe that I have seen declares that a serviceable ink can be made from mild or watered-down vinegar mixed with soot. Nevertheless, I doubt such a product as this would have had much staying quality.

It is known that Spanish officials and churchmen occasionally had silver ink wells on their desks. But on the Southwestern frontier such luxuries were fairly rare. Most people in those days used an inkhorn. That was a hollowed out deer antler with a wooden plug. Dry grains of ink were carried in it and when you wanted to write it was only necessary to add a little saliva or water.

Spanish explorers who crisscrossed the plains and deserts generally carried inkhorns because they were so handy. Ink was needed daily to prepare the official log of their expeditions.

At the desk, colonial writers kept a small box of fine sand, which the Spaniards called *arenilla*. As the page was written, it would be sprinkled with the sand to soak up excess wet ink. That was done since blotting paper had not yet come into use.

If you have stayed with me to this point, you've probably learned more about Spanish ink than you ever wanted to know. But to make your knowledge complete, I must add a word about pens.

The Spaniards, like most other Europeans, used quill pens. The best ones were made from the tail feathers of geese. Such a pen is not very durable and has to be replaced every day or so. There is a story, though, that author Sir Walter Scott wrote an entire novel with one strong goose quill from the Hudson Bay area of Canada.

Cutting a quill just right to form a writing pen is very much an art. The job was done with a small blade that is still known as a "penknife." If the Spaniards of New Mexico had any special techniques for sharpening quills, they failed to record it.

Signature of Don Antonio de Otermin, governor of New Mexico during the Pueblo Revolt of 1680. (From the collection of Marc Simmons)

There exists some dispute over just when and where the first metal pen points were invented. In America, anyway, it was a Baltimore shoemaker who took out the first patent in 1809 for a "metallic writing pen." Within a few years after that date, they were fairly common in the East.

Joab Houghton, coming over the Santa Fe Trail in 1843, gets credit with introducing steel pen points to New Mexico. But in remote parts of the Territory, goose quills continued in service almost to the end of the century. When President Taft signed the New Mexico state-hood bill in 1912, he used a quill pen—from an eagle captured at Taos.

One other writing trick that dates from the colonial period involves the pencil. Spanish settlers and soldiers took a lead musket ball, sharpened a point on it, and had a crude but effective pencil. And there we have a perfect illustration of the old proverb: "Necessity is the mother of invention."

Playing-Cards

✥

No one can say with certainty where playing-cards originated, but they are thought to have come from the Far East along with paper money and gunpowder. The Moors probably brought decks of cards and the game of chess to Spain sometime in the Middle Ages.

America's conquistadors loved to gamble, and we know that when Cortés marched through Mexico in 1520 his men carried packs of cards. They spent their evenings slapping them down by the light of campfires and wagering the piles of treasure looted from the Indians. The Aztecs, so the early records tell us, watched those games with delight and were fascinated by the brightly colored cards.

It seems that colonists with the 1598 colonizing expedition of Juan de Oñate brought the first decks to the upper Rio Grande Valley. Later, traders from Chihuahua included cards among the small assortment of luxury goods offered to New Mexicans. The merchants purchased them initially from the Spanish government which held a monopoly on the printing and sale of playing-cards. Revenue derived from this business went into the royal treasury.

The eye-catching Spanish deck contains forty cards. The suit symbols are swords, cups, coins, and clubs. The eights, nines, and tens are left out. Also, following Oriental custom there is no queen. Taking her place is a knight, or caballero. He is one of the three "court cards" that includes a king and a page. Each of these figures wears a flashy costume typical of the dress once seen at the royal court in Madrid.

Today several museums in the Southwest have in their collections decks of cards made by the Apaches. They were copied from the Spaniards. These cards are made of rawhide with designs crudely painted on by hand. The dress of the king, knight, and page was meaningless to the Indians, so they substituted typical Apache costumes.

The favorite game of days gone by was Mexican monte, a game like faro in which players bet against the dealer, or banker. Anybody who owned a deck could spread a blanket on the ground and set himself up as a dealer. When Americans first entered New Mexico in large numbers after 1821, they were surprised to find monte games going on night and day in the plazas of Santa Fe, Albuquerque, and El Paso. Many of them succumbed to gambling fever and promptly lost their wallets.

In the winter of 1850, a pack of cards was respon-

On top, Spanish playing cards and, beneath them, Apache cards adapted from them. (From the collection of Marc Simmons)

sible for an Indian massacre. A large party of New Mexican militia had left the settlements and gone west to fight the Navajo. When troops found that enemy scouts had learned of their advance, they decided to give up the campaign and make a hasty retreat to the Rio Grande.

On the way home, the commander discovered that a Navajo war party was following in the distance, hoping to pick off any stragglers. So for safety, he warned his companions to stay close together. A group of about

33

a dozen men, however, violated orders. Eager to see their families, they slipped away and headed for their village.

That night they camped in a canyon, built a large campfire to keep away the cold, and posted a guard. Someone produced a deck of cards and a hot game of monte was soon in progress. If the New Mexicans had not become so engrossed in their gambling, they might have noticed the growing nervousness of the horses or the frequent hooting of owls in the darkness around camp. When the game finally broke up at a late hour, they fell exhausted into their blankets and were soon snoring.

Just before dawn, the dozing guard suddenly tumbled over with an arrow in his back. The Navajos were among the sleeping forms in an instant, and it was all over.

Several days later, a search party found the bodies. Blood-spattered cards scattered among the yucca by the wind told the grim story.

The Forgotten Dog

✦

E veryone who has even the slightest acquaintance with the history of the Southwest knows that the horse played an important role in the spread of European culture throughout the area. In books, paintings, and sculpture, we are continually reminded of the horse's contribution to the settling of the West. The dog, on the other hand, has been virtually neglected.

Dogs, unlike horses, were native to the New World. Among the Indians they were popular as pets, but more significantly, they served as beasts of burden and as a back-up food supply. They had other uses too. Watch dogs were the best security against surprise attack. They were employed in hunting, running wild game into rivers where the hunter could get a shot with bow and arrows. Some dogs were trained to turn revolving spits with meat over a campfire. And in winter time, they were always in demand as foot warmers in the Indian bed.

Early Spaniards visiting the Pueblo villages in the Rio Grande valley found them well stocked with canines. The animals were usually described as small and shaggy in appearance, quite different from those accompanying the explorers. One soldier in the 1580s wrote that the Indians even had dog houses. He referred to them as "small underground huts." Perhaps they were not dog houses at all, but actually pit ovens which provided shelter for the animals when not needed for baking. Today the Pueblo people cover the doorways of their outdoor adobe ovens with a slab of stone—to prevent dogs from moving in on cold days.

Archeologists have recovered bones of Indian dogs that date back several thousand years. Two complete natural mummies of prehistoric Basketmaker dogs have been found in dry caves, so we know what the earliest animals looked like. They were small, about cocker spaniel size, and had short noses. One of the mummies wore shaggy hair having a mixed black and white or pinto pattern. The ancient dogs probably ran the full gamut of colors we see on modern mutts.

It wasn't long after the Spaniards introduced their own breeds that the pure Pueblo dog disappeared. The newcomers brought mastiffs and large greyhounds, for hunting purposes but also to overawe the Indians. The bones of a huge greyhound have been excavated at the Spanish mission site of Awatowi among the Hopi Pueblos of northern Arizona.

One curious thing about the Pueblo dogs: they were able to climb up and down the ladders that gave access to the various levels of the Indians' multi-storied build-

A New Mexico shepherd and his dog. (From Samuel Cozzens, *The Marvellous Country* [1876])

ings. It seems likely that they were self-taught, not trained by their owners. As late as the 1880s, an Army lieutenant, visiting Zuni Pueblo in western New Mexico, wrote in amazement of seeing dogs scampering up and down ladders like well-schooled circus performers.

The Apaches, who roamed the southern plains at the coming of the Europeans, possessed a different type of dog from the Pueblos. It was larger and stronger, about the dimensions of a coyote. A member of Coronado's party in 1541 mentions such dogs seen in an

Apache hunting camp. "These people have dogs like ours," he wrote. "They load them as beasts of burden with small pack saddles, cinched with cords. When they are traveling the dogs drag the poles on which the skin tents are packed, a load of perhaps 50 pounds."

What he was viewing, of course, was the travois, poles tied on either side of the dog with their tips allowed to drag on the ground. It was a device the Indians later adapted to the horse and was about the best sort of conveyance for a people who lacked the wheel, if we exclude the dog sled of the Eskimos.

A party of Spaniards, which ventured onto the plains of eastern New Mexico in 1598, encountered an Indian camp on the move. One of the men recorded in his diary: "The Indians use medium-sized dogs which they harness like mules. They have large droves of them, each girt around the breast and haunches, carrying a load of at least 100 pounds. It is interesting to see them traveling along, one after the other, almost all of them with sores under the harness. When the Indian women load these dogs, they hold their heads between their legs, and in this manner load them or straighten the packs."

Aside from these few details, we know very little about how the Apaches and other nomadic tribes trained and handled their dogs.

With the growth of Spanish settlements along the Rio Grande, the dog population of New Mexico prospered. Travelers never failed to mention the swarms of yelping, tumbling canines that greeted them at every village and farm.

The New Mexicans, it seems, had their own breed

of sheep dog, nimble and well-trained. For moving and herding the flocks and protecting them from predators, this dog was indispensible. In gathering sheep, or goats and cattle for that matter, he was said to be the equal of three men on horseback in rough country.

Before Supermarkets

W ho doesn't love a market or a fair? In practically every age and every country, people have come together at appointed times to buy and sell. Such gatherings not only join merchant and customer, they open opportunities for visiting, exchange of news, and impromptu games and races. Country boy and country maid, meeting at a town market, have produced untold romances through time.

No one can say exactly when the first market or fair was held in New Mexico. The earliest Spaniards found that the Pueblos were accustomed to travel up and down the Rio Grande with wares on their backs and that Apaches sometimes walked in from the plains with a few paltry things to barter. But in those hard, far-off days, surpluses were few and little reason existed to develop market places.

All that changed with the Spanish settlement of New Mexico. The newcomers brought with them a dazzling array of trade goods: beads, mirrors, cloth, awls, knives, hatchets, needles, scissors, bells, and a hundred other novel things eagerly snapped up by the Native Americans. The Spaniards also introduced new crops and livestock of all kinds, which found a ready sale among Indian farmers.

It was the appearance and spread of the horse, though, which led directly to an economic revolution and produced the first of the great colonial fairs. When the plains and mountain tribes on the outskirts of New Mexico acquired horses, they discovered that their days of famine and poverty were over. Now they could bring down all the buffalo, deer, and elk they wanted. Extra hides and jerked meat gave them valuable trade commodities, which could be easily carried on horseback to buyers in the Rio Grande valley. And the new mobility allowed them to raid their distant enemies—the Pawnee, the Osage, and the Wichita—and bring back captives and stolen horses, also salable to the New Mexicans and Pueblos.

This new and promising commerce led to the first fair—possibly sometime in the middle 1600s and probably in the Taos Valley. The story is sketchy, because local records kept by the Spaniards were destroyed at the time of the Pueblo Revolt in 1680. Later, after 1710 or so, fairs attended by Spaniards, Pueblos, and nomads began to pop up all over New Mexico.

A yearly fair was held at old Pecos Pueblo, mainly for the convenience of the Plains Apache. Santa Clara Pueblo sponsored another to attract the Navajo and Ute. The Navajo also attended a fair at Jemez Pueblo, and occasionally one at Laguna. Far to the south, the Mes-calero Apache rode in December to a huge fair at El Paso del Norte, held by the Spaniards in conjunction with the feast of Guadalupe.

But the granddaddy of all New Mexican fairs was the one celebrated in October, after the fall harvest, at Taos. In size, color, pageantry, noise, and violence the great Taos fair was unrivaled.

By all accounts, the Taos fair got off to a shaky start. In the forepart of the century, the Spanish governors at Santa Fe prohibited common citizens from attending the fair, mainly as a way to monopolize the valuable trade for themselves and their friends. The infuriated colo-nists, however, appealed to the missionaries who smug-gled letters to Mexico City with word of this travesty. As a result, a royal order came from on high, proclaim-ing the fairs open to everyone.

That must have happened about 1723, the year when another government edict formally established the Taos fair as the chief trading event for all the plains and mountain tribes. The document merely gave legal rec-ognition to what was already an acknowledged fact.

The appearance and development of a genuine fair at Taos lured the business-minded like a magnet. The often-observed fondness of the Pueblo people for trad-ing was matched by a similar devotion on the part of Comanches, Navajos, Utes, and Apaches. Nor was the attachment to barter any less strong among the Euro-pean settlers. One has only to glance backward to mother Spain and recall the glitter of the many fairs of the fif-teenth and sixteenth centuries, especially the huge in-ternational fair at Medina del Campo, to understand that

A Pueblo Indian trader at the Fair in Taos. (From "Account of Disorders in New Mexico, 1778")

the Spaniard has an inborn love for the hurly-burly of such goings-on.

To the affair at Taos, the royal government contributed a feature that dated back to Roman times in Western Europe. That was the so-called peace of the market, sometimes referred to as "the truce of God"—a general agreement that all persons going to and from a fair should be accorded safe conduct. Many Indian groups were familiar with the concept, having a similar practice, so that it was fairly easy to impose a rule that merchants bound for Taos enjoyed freedom from attack.

That was crucial to the success of the fair, since the

nomadic tribes just mentioned were often at war with one another, and just as often engaged in hostilities with the Spaniards and Pueblos. The truce of God was not a perfect shield, being imperfectly observed, but within broad parameters it imposed enough order on bands of volatile traders to allow an unexpected measure of security. Yet, under the surface of each fair there lurked the potential for a fiery explosion.

In a bid to prevent that very thing, the governor at Santa Fe, accompanied by a soldier escort and packloads of personal trade goods, usually journeyed to Taos for the duration of the fair. As the official party approached its destination, it encountered other groups, Indian and Spanish, converging from all directions. The floodtide of people seemed to engulf the level ground surrounding Taos Pueblo, which was the site of the fair. Up went teepees, tents, and stalls.

Haggling and swapping went on day and night. So too did drinking bouts, horseraces, and amorous encounters between local girls and the visitors. Nine months after a fair, there was always a rash of births. The Taos Indians referred to the infants, in their own language, as "grass babies." A priest who witnessed the fair in 1761 wrote that the scene was so wild and unchaste that he was embarrassed to speak of it.

At each fair the overriding question was always: What is the mood of the Comanches? Members of the tribe were among the most important participants in the trade, but their surliness and tendency to fly-off-the-handle made them much feared. One year, for example, some Comanches had a batch of captive women to sell. When no one showed interest, they became enraged and butchered the hapless ladies in the midst of the market ground. The King of Spain, upon hearing of the episode, was so grieved that he ordered creation of a special mercy fund so that Indian captives brought to the Taos fair could be ransomed and raised as Christians.

Unfortunately, as some sober-minded colonists observed, the King's humanitarian gesture merely expanded the problem. The Comanches stepped up efforts to collar captives, knowing that all would be ransomed at Taos, while the settlers had a cheap source of labor delivered into their hands. In this lay one of the tragic sides of the Taos fair.

Strictly speaking, the Spanish New Mexicans were prevented by law from owning Indian slaves. But they could take plains captives into their homes as "servants" and teach them the ways of civilized Christians. This practice had received official sanction back in the 1690s.

By the end of the colonial period and the opening of the Santa Fe Trail from Missouri in 1821, the fairs at Taos, Pecos, Jemez, and other outlying communities were already in decline. With caravans of Pittsburg wagons arriving from the East and traveling downriver to Chihuahua, the cities of Santa Fe, Albuquerque, and El Paso became the principal centers of commerce.

In the 1830s, Santa Fe was conducting a regular trade fair in July whenever the first wagon train of the season showed up. In addition to the fair, residents of the capital patronized a local market held daily on the main plaza. Under porches surrounding the square, an abundant variety of local foodstuffs and handcrafts were offered to the public.

Attorney William W. H. Davis visited the Santa Fe market in the 1850s and described what he saw. "At the west end of the Governors Palace the country people sell their meats, fruits and vegetables they carry to town. In the winter Indians bring in fine venison and wild turkeys. Now and then the carcass of a large bear is exposed for sale. The meats are hung up on a line made fast to two posts of the porch, while the vegetables are put on little mats or pieces of board on the ground. Beside them the vender will sit and wait for customers with a patience that seems to rival Job. And if they do not sell out today, they are sure to return with the same stock tomorrow."

Nearly a hundred and fifty years after Mr. Davis wrote, the Pueblo people still journey to Santa Fe each day to spread their wares in the same spot. Now they come by pickup instead of burro, and they sell mostly items for the tourist trade. But in the autumn after the harvest, melons and chiles, colored corn and bread appear alongside the piles of souvenirs just as in times past.

The special two-day Indian market that overflows the entire plaza each August has some of the spirit of the old colonial fairs—even though the mayhem and promiscuity are missing. Indians of many tribes display their finest products. People mill about and gossip. There is much laughter and spicy native food. And hardly anyone is aware that he is helping to perpetuate a tradition whose roots go far back into the economic history of New Mexico.

Slave Raiding

✤

A tragic side of New Mexico history is the long story of Indian slavery. Even before permanent settlers came in 1598, Spanish slavers from the mining towns of northern Mexico raided native villages along the Rio Grande.

During the next century, unscrupulous governors at Santa Fe rounded up Indian captives and sold them into slavery in Chihuahua. Soon, too, wealthy ranchers in New Mexico began to accumulate numerous Indian women and children as household servants. These were really slaves since they had been purchased.

In many towns between El Paso and Taos, captives were sold after church on Sundays in the plaza. A strong eight-year-old girl sometimes brought as much as $400. Boys were not much wanted because they tended to run

Laguna Pueblo was a stopping place for slavers on their way to the Navajo country. (From the New Mexico Department of Development)

away at the first opportunity. Girls, however, more easily became attached to their owner's family.

The village of Cebolleta in western New Mexico became a center of the slave trade, its men specializing in this unsavory business. They engaged in hundreds of raids on encampments of the Navajos whose country lay just to the west.

Whenever a rich *don* on the Rio Grande was preparing for the wedding of a daughter, he would send his agent to Cebolleta with funds to purchase a female Navajo slave. That slave would be presented to his offspring as a marriage gift.

This traffic was not one-sided. The Navajos themselves raided New Mexican households and carried off children and young women to perform domestic service or herd sheep. Occasionally, the captives escaped and made their way home over hundreds of miles, with harrowing stories to tell. But usually they remained with the tribe and grew up as Navajos.

New Mexico's first territorial governor, James S. Calhoun, had this to say about the practice: "The trading in captives has been so long tolerated in this Territory that it has ceased to be regarded as a wrong." Although widely accepted at the time, slave raiding by any standard has to be regarded as one of the great evils of frontier society. The horrors that it produced are suggested by an account a Hopi elder recorded in 1925. He recalled as a boy witnessing a raid by New Mexicans on his own village of Oraibi (in northern Arizona) about 1864.

The Cebolletans and other professional slavers did not often attack the peaceful Hopi, but sometimes they did if no Navajo captives were to be found. On this occasion a large company of New Mexicans, heavily armed, rode into Oraibi and camped.

The two-week long winter solstice ceremony was in full progress and the entire Oraibi priesthood was in the underground kiva making sacred prayer sticks. It was the duty of the married women to make paper bread, called *piki*, and carry it to the priests for their meal.

Many Indians were on the rooftops watching as the women moved toward the kiva with their bread. The New Mexicans had built a fire there and were warming their hands. As the women approached they took the bread from them and ate it. Then they began loading their guns.

49

Panic quickly spread through the village. Women and children began to run as gunfire started at the kiva. Several priests trying to exit by their ladder were shot. The slavers dashed about snatching children and then herding them out of Oraibi. When they had gone, families emerged wailing, knowing their youngsters had been abducted.

The Oraibi leaders held a council and decided to send a delegation to meet with the American chief (governor) in Santa Fe. The Hopis did confront the governor and demanded the return of their children. It took some doing since the captive waifs were by now scattered over much of New Mexico. But eventually they were all found and sent to the Indian agent at Keams Canyon in the Hopi country.

The agent gave each child new clothes and a blanket and then sent them home. Although there was much rejoicing in Oraibi, it was tempered by memory of the six Hopis who had been killed in the raid.

Indian slavery was made illegal by a presidential proclamation issued in 1865. But for some years after that the practice continued in secret. As late as the 1930s there were still Indian women living in Hispanic households who had been captured from their tribe as children.

Naturally, they were no longer slaves but they had been with the family so long, as a servant, that they had no wish to leave, or for that matter any place else to go.

Apache Exiles

⚜

Throughout the colonial period in northern Mexico, the Apaches remained the bitterest and most unyielding foes of the Spaniards. The royal government spent literally millions of pesos in a futile effort to subdue the tribe and make the northern frontier safe for settlement.

In the beginning, padres attempted to convert the Apaches and win them over by peaceful means. When that failed, the Spanish government erected a string of military presidios reaching from the Gulf of Mexico to the Sea of Cortés. But the thin line of forts and the campaigns mounted from them proved no barrier at all to wandering Indian war parties.

In desperation, about 1770 officials adopted a new policy that they hoped ultimately would resolve the Apache problem. They began deporting Indians from the frontier, sending them south in chain gangs, first to Mexico City and later to Havana.

Clamped in leg irons and chained together, they were shipped south with the first wagon train passing down the Camino Real. According to Spanish documents it appears that Indian prisoners from New Mexico and west Texas were assembled at the Presidio of San Elizario in the valley below El Paso. When enough of them had been brought in, they were marched, clanking chains and all, on the long road toward Mexico City.

The trip must have been a nightmare. The Indians realized they were heading for a life of slavery and would probably never see their homeland and families again. Some always died from exhaustion along the way, and occasionally smallpox broke out killing the entire party.

But the spirit of the Apaches was unbreakable and attempts to escape were frequent. Quite often, half the captives would be women who were known to be as fierce warriors as the men. As a result, the escort of Spanish soldiers took the tightest precautions to maintain security.

One group of prisoners in 1799 was made up entirely of Indian women, fifty-one in all. The troops called a halt one night at an inn and locked their charges in a large room. Just before dawn, the women broke out, attacked and injured several guards, and made good their escape.

In Mexico City, the Apaches were distributed to households of leading Spaniards where they served as domestic slaves. Increasingly after 1780, however, the Indians would slip off, and traveling nights through unfamiliar country, eventually made their way 3,000 kilometers north to join their people. Having suffered un-

52

Warm Springs Apaches (called Ojo Calientes by the Spaniards) of southern New Mexico were exiled to Cuba in the eighteenth century. (From Museum of New Mexico, neg. no. 16372)

told hardships and also learned about the customs of the Spaniards, these fugitives became dangerous leaders in the continuing war on the northern frontier.

To stop the flight of the Indians from captivity, the government decided to send them to Cuba. The island was already a dumping ground for military deserters, beggars, gamblers, and similar undesirable elements from other parts of Spanish America. The Apaches, after debarking, were set to work on plantations or on fortifications being built in the port of Havana.

The Spaniards assumed that the long sea journey to Cuba and the impossibility of returning home would destroy the Indians' spirit of resistance. But they figured wrong. Unless kept under constant guard, the captives broke their irons and fled to the hills in the interior. From there, they carried out raids much as they had once done in their homeland. How strange the war cry of desert Apaches must have sounded in the tropical forests of the Caribbean.

Royal troops pursued the Indians relentlessly. They feared that their example might inspire Black slaves on the plantations to launch a revolt. Whenever cornered, the Apaches usually fought to the death, knowing that surrender meant a return to the chain gangs.

In 1790, the Spaniards discovered that they had committed a mistake in exiling one fourteen-year-old Apache boy. He had been picked up the year before wandering in the mountains near the headwaters of the Gila River. Later, they learned that he was the son of a chief of a small band that had made peace.

An order went out to military officials throughout Mexico and Cuba instructing them to check all Apache prisoners to see if they could find the lad. The government hoped to make amends by returning him to his father. But, in spite of their best efforts, he was never found. Likely, he had died somewhere by the side of the road and, unchained from his companions, been buried in an unmarked grave.

The Sabinal Apaches

✦

During three centuries of exploring and settling in the Southwest, colonial Spaniards were constantly at war with their Indian neighbors. But that was not the way they wanted it. Time and again the Spanish government sent its armies against the hostile tribes in a bid to win peace on the battlefield. But when that failed, as it often did, diplomacy was tried. By the mid 1780s, a combination of force and peaceful persuasion had brought the Comanche, Navajo and Ute to terms. Only the Apache of southern New Mexico were left to be defeated.

Spanish soldiers could now turn their full attention to that end. And they had the help of the newly won Comanches who were age-old foes of the Apaches. There was no question in anyone's mind that the Apache Indians were dangerous and able opponents. In 1786, for example, a Mescalero war party rode 2,000 miles south to carry out raids around Guadalajara and Mexico City. It returned months later without the loss of a man!

The Spanish campaigns launched against the tribe in the late 1780s proved devastating, however. Troop movements out of Chihuahua, Sonora, and southern New Mexico caught them in a vise. The Apaches, for several years straight, suffered a string of defeats.

By late 1789, at least some of the Indians were ready to sue for peace. With both the Spanish and Comanche arrayed against them, not even the remotest mountains offered sanctuary. The royal governor at Santa Fe, Don Fernando de la Concha, was delighted. But he was also wary. Could the Apaches be trusted?

To the Indian envoys that came to him from the Mimbres Mountains in the southwest and the Sierra Blanca Mountains in the southeast, the governor set a stern condition. The Apache tribesmen would be on probation for six months. No military expeditions would be sent against them and if they kept the peace, a formal treaty would be arranged. But if the truce was broken, then it was back to total war.

Surprisingly, the agreement held and in the spring of 1790 a befeathered host of Apache chiefs traveled northward to Santa Fe. There they made peace with Governor Concha.

Among other things, they agreed never again to raid the town of El Paso (then part of New Mexico), or the frontiers of Chihuahua and Sonora. They also promised to settle down at some spot on the Rio Grande and take up farming. For his part, the governor guaranteed them seed, tools, and Spanish workers to help get their farms started.

The Spaniards considered the entire thing an experiment—one that would determine if the warlike Apache were capable of giving up their roaming ways and settling down to live like Europeans and the Pueblo Indians. It was a novel idea for the time.

The place Concha selected for his experimental Indian town was at Sabinal on the Rio Grande between Belen and Socorro. There were a few colonists living scattered about, but most of the land was empty and waiting for the plow.

Over the next few months, the Indians began to drift into Sabinal and pitch camp. Governor Concha himself came down from Santa Fe and with the aid of local Spanish residents showed the Apaches how to dig irrigation ditches and clear fields. While the work was going forward, rations of corn and meat were issued.

The governor also sent an order to Spaniards in Albuquerque and Bernalillo to take up a collection of money, which would be used to build houses for the Indians. And he directed that they also contribute cattle to help form an Apache herd.

The project and the way it was carried out seem truly extraordinary! Only a short time before the two peoples had been engaged in bitter warfare. Now the colonists were not only welcoming their old enemies into their midst, they were contributing labor and money in a bid for their friendship. It was something that would have been wholly unthinkable on the American frontier.

The Indians who occupied the new town became known as the Sabinal Apaches. They were drawn mostly from the Mescalero and Warm Springs (or *Ojo Caliente*) bands. Actually not all the Mescaleros came in. A few remained hidden out in the mountains, and at least one

Ancestors of Apaches like these were settled at Sabinal by the Spaniards in the 1790s. (From the collection of Marc Simmons)

group appears to have settled on the outskirts of El Paso, receiving a welcome similar to that of their Sabinal cousins farther north.

Governor Concha, enthusiastic about the initial success of his plans, returned to Sabinal in the spring of 1793. By then, the Indians were living in two settlements on opposite banks of the river and they had large fields under cultivation.

At that time they asked permission, and the governor granted it, to leave for several weeks to gather the spiny mescal plant on the deserts to the south. The sweet mescal was one of their favorite foods, and, in fact, it gave the Mescaleros their name.

Unfortunately, the experiment, which for three years had looked so promising, was soon to fall apart. The governor, suffering from a severe eye ailment, left New Mexico for the army hospital in Chihuahua. His disability turned out to be permanent and he never returned to his post.

The governorship passed to Fernando de Chacón, a man far less energetic than his predecessor and one who showed little concern for the struggling effort at Sabinal. The Apaches, without encouragement from Santa Fe, quickly lost interest in hoeing and plowing. Gradually they drifted back to their old nomadic life and by the end of the century they were once again at war with the New Mexicans.

For many years the ruins of their communities at Sabinal stood on the banks of the Rio Grande as a mute reminder of Governor Concha's noble enterprise. Then, in 1856 the river overflowed its banks and buried the walls, fields, and ditches under several feet of silt. And the Sabinal experiment was almost completely forgotten.

On Guard

✤

The late Dr. Bainbridge Bunting of the University of New Mexico was our leading authority on early architecture in the state. In a series of fine books, he outlined the history of building in New Mexico. One topic he mentioned only in passing was that of watchtowers built by colonial New Mexicans.

Those watchtowers have always fascinated me. They were used by the Spaniards, not only as look-out positions, but also as defensive strongholds. On the New Mexico frontier, many a furious battle took place around their curved walls.

For centuries watchtowers had been a standard feature of castles established along the Spanish coast. From them, soldiers watched the sea for any sign of Turkish or Moorish pirates. And if the castle was attacked, the tower became a rallying point for defenders.

It was only natural, I suppose, that the Spaniards should take the idea of towers with them to the New World. Fairly early in Mexico, towers show up on both public and private buildings.

Some of those on the coast continued to be used as look-outs for pirates. But inland, the tower became a center of defense against hostile Indians. Examples, perfectly preserved, can still be found attached to some of the large colonial haciendas in northern Mexico.

Then, of course, the Spaniards brought towers with them to the upper Rio Grande Valley. The ones built here, called *torreones,* were on a far smaller scale than the massive watchtowers attached to Spanish castles.

The average New Mexican tower was a round, two-story structure made of adobe and rock. Walls were two to three feet thick and the diameter of the interior only about fifteen feet. Sometimes there was a small fireplace for winter heating and cooking. A trap door in the ceiling led to the upper level, reached by a ladder.

During an emergency, women and children crowded into the lower room. Men took to the upper story where they could fire at attackers through slits or loopholes. The *torreon* was not made for a long siege. In fact, Father Francisco Domínguez in 1776 referred to it as a death trap.

Most of the New Mexican towers were built as single units, unattached to other structures. They were placed in small villages that had nothing else for defense, or in areas where several farms lay close together. At the first sign of trouble, people scooped up their children and headed for the torreon. When it was not in use, which was most of the time, the tower served as a storeroom for crops.

A defensive *torreon* as part of a hacienda at Manzano, New Mexico. (From the collection of Marc Simmons)

There are references in early documents to larger, more impressive towers. The Spanish Governor's Palace at Santa Fe once had a substantial tower at each end of the building. For a while, the one on the east end served as a temporary chapel. And well into the nineteenth century, the west tower doubled as a jail. Both have long since disappeared.

In the 1770s when Comanche raids were at their peak, the Indians of Taos raised torreones, in the Spanish style, for protection. Father Domínguez referred to the village in these terms: "Its plan resembles that of those walled cities with bastions and towers that are described to us in the Bible." The padre goes on to note five fortified towers built into the walls.

Nowhere in New Mexico today does an original and complete torreon survive. The lower story of one still stands in the village of Talpa near Taos. And partial remains of others can occasionally be found here and there. A fine example at Manzano near Albuquerque was demolished by the State Highway Department in 1939 when it widened the road.

There are, however, at least two nice reconstructions. One tower of adobe has been restored at the Old Cienega Village Museum (el Rancho de las Golondrinas) south of Santa Fe. The other restored torreon is at Lincoln.

That tower was started soon after 1850 when settlers from the Rio Grande moved east and took up homes along the Rio Bonito. Even with their torreon for defense the people around Lincoln were driven out three times by the Indians.

After the raids stopped, the tower was neglected and fell into ruin. It did figure briefly in the events surrounding the Lincoln County War. By the early 1930s, only about five feet of the walls still stood. But later, the torreon was restored and it is now a prime tourist attraction in Lincoln.

Enough to Eat

⚜

S peaking of agricultural conditions in New Mexico, one of the missionary friars who came with Juan de Oñate in 1598 declared solemnly: "Here, corn is God."

By that, he meant, of course, that getting enough to eat was the largest problem faced by the first European settlers in the Southwest. Oñate himself expected to make a quick silver strike, which he believed would lead to the development of a major mining and smelting industry. But until that occurred, he knew that his colonists would have to be supported by their own farming and pastoral enterprises. To that end, he had been careful to include seeds and livestock in the inventory of his expedition.

The silver bonanza never materialized, so that in later years agriculture and stock raising became the twin mainstays of New Mexico's colonial economy. Before they were fully established, however, the Spaniards experienced a period of food scarcity, during which their needs were met by exacting tribute in corn from the Pueblos.

Although the Pueblo Indians possessed extensive fields, covering most of the arable land between Socorro and the Española Valley, their assembly of crops was comparatively small. Their only major food plants were corn, beans, and squash, each in several varieties. To these were added two nonfood crops, cotton and gourds.

By all accounts of the Spanish chroniclers, the Pueblos were careful to keep several years' surplus of foodstuffs in storerooms, as a hedge against crop failure and famine. But even so, they were scarcely prepared to provide the quantities of grain demanded by Oñate's people.

The Spaniards, for their part, looked to the planting of fields almost from the first moment of their arrival. At San Juan Pueblo, where they initially settled, irrigation ditches were dug and crops sown, even before construction of a church commenced. Evidently, the newcomers drafted Indian labor from San Juan and neighboring pueblos for much of this work.

The crops, introduced by the first Spaniards, included wheat and barley, as well as a variety of other plants, *traídas de Castilla* ("brought from Castile"). In the latter category, we find reference to such foods as cabbage, onions, lettuce, radishes, cantaloupes, and watermelons. Grape vines and fruit trees seem to have arrived later.

With Oñate also came crops native to Mexico, which had not been grown before on the upper Rio Grande. Among this group were chile, cultivated tobacco, Mex-

A field of bearded Spanish barley at Ranchos de Taos. (From the collection of Marc Simmons)

ican varieties of beans, and the tomato. Moreover, the Spaniards brought new types of corn from the south, previously unknown to Pueblo farmers. One of those was a variety called *Cristolina de Chihuahua*, characterized by a long, large cob and possibly by grains that were predominantly white.

It is thought to have cross-pollinated rapidly with all the native Pueblo corns (except the pop corn), producing a hybrid that greatly increased local yields. A bit later in the colonial period, the Spaniards introduced the many-rowed Mexican Dent, ancestor of the modern

Corn Belt Dent. It too had a profound impact on the corn of the Rio Grande Pueblos, contributing to the extremely long cobs so noticeable in the native product today.

The effect upon Pueblo farming of all these introductions, both Old World and American, was profound. The new crops intensified agricultural productivity, expanded the need for arable land, provided relief from failure of prehistoric cultivars, and helped diversify the native diet. But benefits to the Indians, in the beginning at least, werely largely offset by other problems associated with Spanish occupation of the area.

One of the chief problems facing the settlers throughout the colonial years was the scarcity of land suitable for tilling. The most fertile soil lay in the principal stream and river valleys, and there, too, could be found the only large and reliable source of water available for ditch irrigation. Such lowlands, however, comprised only about 1 percent of the total land area of the province. And most of that, within the upper Rio Grande drainage, was already under cultivation by the Pueblos.

Spanish colonial law was strict in prohibiting anyone from encroaching upon lands of the Indians. Indeed, it is assumed that Oñate's first settlers usurped fields belonging to San Juan Pueblo and that, at least in part, it was the slow-moving wheels of the legal system which obliged them in 1609 or early 1610 to move southward to the, then, unoccupied valley of the Santa Fe River.

As Pueblo population steadily declined during the colonial years—owing principally to warfare, famine, and pestilence—irrigable farms were left vacant and could be reassigned to Spaniards under the laws regulating land grants. Nevertheless, the European population expanded so rapidly, particularly in the last half century of the period, that finding enough cropland to answer the agricultural needs of settlers remained an acute problem.

Shortage or not, colonial farmers early discovered that lands which they *could* put to the plow amply rewarded their labor. Speaking of New Mexico, Fray Alonso de Benavides declared in 1634 that, "This land . . . is the most abundant and fertile of all the Indies . . . and produces an incredible quantity." His earnest, if somewhat exaggerated, remark was echoed more than a century later by Governor Thomas Vélez Cachupín who credited the province with being the most fertile of all New Spain, although he noted, perhaps with some perturbation, that the Pueblos, not the Spaniards, owned the richest soil.

The farmlands of the Rio Grande Valley were, in effect, auto-replenishing through the agency of silt-laden irrigation and flood waters. Before installation of flood-control dams above Albuquerque, the river carried an estimated 75 billion pounds of sediment annually. As the flow of water from irrigation ditches spread across the surface of cultivated fields, it released its heavy burden of silt, leaving, according to a Spanish colonist in 1773, "a thick mud which serves as manure for the land . . . a glutinous scum resembling lard." This sediment accumulated at the rate of about one-quarter of an inch a year on cropland.

Periodic flooding by the Rio Grande and its tributaries, while destructive to farm installations and homes, also contributed to restoring soil fertility through deposition of alluvium. This material was rich in mineral

69

nutrients and organic matter washed from the forested and heavily grassed slopes of the mountains. The benefits to soil thus bestowed led a nineteenth-century American traveler to pronounce the "Valley of the Rio Grande as productive as the Valley of the Nile."

While colonial farmers could praise the richness of their soil, they must have had trouble in finding anything favorable to say about the weather. That was because a climatic period known as the Little Ice Age, extending from about A.D. 1450 to 1850, brought colder temperatures to most parts of the Northern hemisphere.

Although no statistical climatic data is available for New Mexico in the colonial era, numerous references by contemporary observers convey a qualitative picture of the weather experienced by Spaniards on the upper Rio Grande. That view incorporates such elements as severe temperatures in winter, excessive snowfall, late thaws and early frosts, and regular freezing of the Rio Grande. The net result was a lowering of agricultural potential owing to a shortening of the growing season.

The frigid winters and unseasonal frosts must have caused crop failure with some frequency. Orchards and vineyards were especially vulnerable to hard freezes that lingered far into spring. Young field crops, withered by late frosts, could be replanted, with the farmer gambling that enough time remained for them to mature.

Historians have tended to overlook the harmful impact which the Little Ice Age had upon colonial New Mexico's economy. There can be no doubt that on the practice of farming alone, it placed a considerable strain. Governor Alberto Maynez, writing from Santa Fe just six years before independence, declared that New Mexico was in a miserable state because "the extreme cold has proven the ruination of agriculture and stock raising." While the governor may have overstated the case, his remark nonetheless was founded on a sincere belief that the weather was hurting the economy.

In addition to a shortage of land and a severe climate, there were other factors inhibiting New Mexico's agricultural development. Governor Fernando de Chacón mentioned two of them in a report prepared in 1803. For one, he claimed that farming methods practiced in his province were very backward. To remedy that, he asked the government to supply him with agricultural manuals showing the latest methods of planting and field care, techniques of insect control, and procedures for grafting. And two, Chacón complained that there was no incentive for the people to engage in commercial agriculture. Owing to the vast distances separating them from major markets in the south, most New Mexicans engaged in subsistence farming, producing little or no surplus. Therefore, in years of bad harvests many of them were reduced to eating wild plants and roots and to slaughtering their livestock just to survive.

The Pueblo Indians, by contrast, were more industrious and better prepared. The governor lauded their practice of working large fields in common; setting aside a portion of the harvest for widows, orphans, and the disabled; and keeping enough surplus on hand to carry them through a series of poor years. In fact, the well-stocked Pueblo granaries had long attracted buyers from the Hispanic community. From them, the presidial quartermaster at Santa Fe was accustomed to purchase grain for the royal troops. And in times of crop failure, civilians sometimes obtained grain from the Indians to see them through the winter.

71

Indian corn, or maize, remained the principal crop to the end of the colonial period. Wheat, a cold-weather grain introduced by the Spaniards, adapted well to the high Taos and Peñasco valleys where the short growing season often prevented corn from reaching maturity. Barley was of minor importance and, as in Spain, it was probably used mainly for livestock feed. Oats and rye, so far as is known, were not grown in colonial New Mexico.

Other field crops included the *frijol* bean, horse bean, peas, squashes and pumpkins, melons, chile, tobacco, and cotton. Only a limited variety of garden vegetables seem to have been cultivated in the later colonial period. Onions and garlic were regarded as staples in the diet, but other things, such as cucumbers, lettuce, beets, and the small husk tomato are mentioned in the documents only rarely. The potato was practically unknown. Several spices—anise, coriander, and possibly saffron—occasionally appeared in kitchen gardens.

Of the orchard crops, apricot, peach, plum, apple, pear, and quince are the ones the Spaniards were able to establish in New Mexico with some success. Figs did not fare well above the El Paso Valley. In 1776, Father Francisco Domínguez indicated that only varieties of fruit resistant to cold were planted north of Santa Fe.

New Mexico's first successful vineyards were established by missionaries of the Socorro district as early as the 1620s. The province produced both wine- and table-grapes. The most common variety reported was the Mission grape. Creditable red and white wines were made, as well as brandy and vinegar.

Significant changes in the basic pattern of farming occurred only after arrival of the railroad in 1880. The importation of new tools and seeds from the East, together with modern practices of cultivation, slowly transformed the face of the rural economy. But even today some Hispanic customs and methods of agriculture can be found among farm communities of northern New Mexico.

Acequias

✤

Almost 400 years ago, Spanish colonists built the first European settlement in the Southwest on the banks of the Rio Grande north of Santa Fe. The spot they selected, near San Juan Pueblo, was surrounded by fertile bottomlands that could be easily irrigated by water from the river. Through long experience in arid Spain and Mexico, those hardy settlers knew that survival would depend on their *acequias,* or ditches. So just as soon as houses and a church were up, they fell to work on an irrigation system.

In later years, as each new town was founded on the Rio Grande, greater demands were made on the river's precious water. Soon after the founding of Albuquerque in 1706, the farmers there put an elaborate web of ditches into operation. Some were so wide and deep according to Father Francisco Domínguez in 1776 that beam bridges had to be installed so that travelers could get across them.

During a visit to New Mexico in 1760, Bishop Pedro Tamarón mentioned a large irrigation ditch at El Paso of such size that it could carry half the waters of the Rio Grande. Secondary canals led from this main ditch, or *acequia madre*, to individual fields. On the river itself, the colonists and Indians working together had constructed a large diversion dam with flood gates. The dam served to deflect a portion of the current into the *acequia madre*.

There was plenty of water for all New Mexican farmers during those years when a heavy snow pack accumulated in the southern Rockies. But like today, the weather tended to run in wet and dry cycles. It took no more than two seasons of drought, back to back, and the settlers faced famine.

During dry spells, small quarrels as well as serious conflicts over water use were common. Some of these ended in court and others led to bloodshed. Generally the people depended on their elected *mayordomo*, or ditch boss, to keep order. It was his job in the spring to call all the villagers together to clean and repair the *acequias*. He also policed the system to make sure no one took more than his allotment of water. In times of shortage, he carefully rationed what was available and assigned hours for each family to open its ditch gates. A farmer often kept his family working all night irrigating the fields to take advantage of every minute allowed by the *mayordomo*.

A number of New Mexico towns in the Rio Grande Valley still retain their old Spanish colonial ditch systems under a *mayordomo*. One of these is Santa Fe. Its *acequia*

The *acequia*, or irrigation ditch, was central to village life. (From Stanley Ward, *Over the Range to the Golden Gate* [1891])

madre winds through the famous artist district above Canyon Road.

The Pueblo Indians also continue many traditional practices regarding irrigation. When explorer Antonio de Espejo traveled through New Mexico in 1583, he wrote in his journal that the Indians had "many irrigated corn fields with canals and dams, built as if by the Spaniards." To their own system, the native people added several practices borrowed from the newcomers, including election of a *mayordomo*. And they have clung to some of their ancient ceremonies right down to the present, among them that of planting prayer sticks in the ditches and holding ritual dances following cleaning of the *acequias* in spring.

Early Spanish farmers knew that the thirsty soil needed water to produce a crop. But they were probably unaware that the silt carried by the irrigation waters was almost as important as the moisture itself. Many early accounts note with some astonishment that Rio Grande farmers never used manure or other fertilizer in their fields. Yet the land continued to yield bountifully year after year. The secret was in the silt, rich in phosphate, potash, and nitrogen, which was deposited each time the field was watered.

As soon as reclamation and flood-control projects began in the twentieth century, that benefit was lost. Dams trapped the silt and the river's water became clear—pleasing to look at, but of less value to cropland.

Silt also served another function. By coating the bottom and sides of irrigation ditches, it made them almost water-tight. Without silt, *acequias* in New Mexico can lose up to 50 percent of their water through seepage. Recently, a number of ditches were paved with concrete along an eighty-mile stretch of the Rio Grande from Albuquerque to Socorro in an effort to prevent such loss. Large sums have been spent to accomplish what the Spaniards got at no cost by letting nature work for them.

Carts
on the Camino Real

⬥

S cholars have paid considerable attention to the political, military and commercial aspects of the Camino Real or Royal Road to Santa Fe, but very little research
has been brought to bear on the technical aspects of the
wheeled vehicles used to carry freight and passengers
over this route. From the founding of New Mexico in
1598 down to Mexican independence in 1821, freight
caravans seasonally traveled from southern cities to the
upper Rio Grande valley. In the seventeenth century,
they took the form of triennial government convoys, the
famous mission-supply trains, referred to as *cuadrillas
de carros*. In the following century, private contractors
organized trains to carry supplies to the Santa Fe presidio, while local New Mexico merchants and ranchers
formed their own protective caravans (*conductas*) to
transport their products to the leading fairs and markets

of the south. This freighting industry, extending over more than two centuries, made use of a distinctive wheeled conveyance: the *carreta*. An examination of its design, manufacture, and use can serve to illuminate a little-known aspect of Hispanic colonial technology.

The carreta was in use for a long period of time. Numerous nineteenth-century visitors to the Southwest left detailed descriptions and a number of examples have survived and are available in collections for study. Apparently, it still saw duty for purely local service in New Mexico as late as the 1890s.

In construction, the carreta was a simple cart body mounted over a few hounds (or braces), an axle, and a pair of wheels. Axles, made of cottonwood or occasionally pine, projected beyond the bed of the cart. Approximately eight inches of the axle at each end were reduced in diameter to form round journals bearing the wheels. The wheels were secured in place by linchpins, which were no more than wooden pegs inserted in holes bored near the extremities of the axle. James F. Meline, touring New Mexico in 1866, noted that carreta axles were prone to break. A plentiful supply of extras, he tells us, was loaded into the cart for any journey beyond a day, so that the carreta was frequently half-filled with them. His statement, no doubt, carries some exaggeration.

Cottonwood was the favored material in the making of carreta wheels. When a tree of sufficient girth could be found, the wheel would be formed from a single section of the trunk. Using no more than an ax and an adze, the wheelwright would trim the outer edges to produce as true a circle as possible. Next he reduced the thickness of the wood, tapering it toward the rim. At

79

the center of the wheel, on both sides, he left hemispherical burrs to serve as the hubs. A hole to receive the axle was pierced through these hubs, either by boring or by using a hot iron.

It seems that in many cases the wheelwright could not find a tree large enough in diameter from which to fashion a one-piece wheel. In that event, he made three separate sections and fitted them together with wooden dowels to create a solid disc. Sometimes two crescent-shaped segments, or felloes, of wood were affixed to the core of a wheel by doweled slats, forming a rough circle and leaving open spaces on the surface of the finished wheel. A refinement almost never seen was "dishing," that is, construction of wheels not in one plane but as a flattened cone. A dished wheel is designed for strength against the sideways thrust inevitable with the swaying of heavy loads. Lacking this, the carreta in motion appeared quite unstable.

Because of its density and resistence to splitting, cottonwood proved to be the best material available for the manufacture of cart wheels. Nevertheless, under the stress of hard use, most wheels soon developed cracks, a condition exacerbated by the dryness of the climate and by occasional wettings experienced in crossing streams. Many carreta wheels now in collections show evidence of patching, usually in the form of wooden mending plates nailed over a split.

In the absence of iron bushings and casings to reinforce the bearing surfaces of the axles and hubs, the hole in the wooden wheel was rapidly enlarged through wear. When this occurred, the carreta wobbled in motion and placed a greater strain on the draft animals.

To cut down on friction, the wheels were sometimes

New Mexico style ox cart, or *carreta*. (From Museum of New Mexico, neg. no. 11826)

greased with buffalo tallow, but more commonly this simple maintenance practice was neglected. Americans coming over the Santa Fe Trail and encountering a train of carretas invariably spoke of the piercing noise of the wheels, describing it as a blood-curdling screech. Typical of early-day comments was that of Lt. John G. Bourke, who said of the carts: "As they rolled over the dusty roads, they squeaked a siren song which wakened the dead for five miles or more." Samuel Woodworth Cozzens added, "The genius who invented the steam-whistle must have obtained the idea from the noise made by the [carreta] wheels."

81

Americans were always astonished that the noisy scream of the cart wheels did not irritate the New Mexicans. Indeed, there is evidence to suggest that this sound, far from displeasing the Hispanic carter and freighter, was actually music to his ears. Peasants in Spain, who employ similar vehicles, refer to them as "singing carts" and speak affectionately of the wheel's soothing, familiar song.

The bed of a carreta, which rested directly on the axle without benefit of springs, had a foundation composed of adzed beams joined by mortise and tenon. A center beam, running the length of the underbody, projected some ten feet beyond the front of the cart and served as the tongue. Flooring for the bed was provided by rough-hewn planks. The superstructure was merely a series of open stakes or undressed poles, each one anchored near the edge of the bed by doweling and joined and braced at the top by a railing, reinforced with rawhide.

Ordinarily the carreta was drawn by one or two yoke of oxen, but more yokes could be added if the load or terrain demanded it. The style of yoke used by carters on the Camino Real was that derived from southern Spain, the horn yoke, which was tied behind the horns with rawhide thongs. With this device the ox had to push with his head and neck, whereas with the collar yoke, which was employed in northern Spain but had not been introduced to the colonies, the animal pulled the load with his shoulders.

This crude, unwieldy carreta with no iron fittings or hardware represents the sort of cart prevalent in New Mexico during the nineteenth century. But documentary evidence suggests that carretas of more skillful construction that were even furnished, at times, with iron tires and iron bushings inside the hubs had been the rule in an earlier day. For long journeys over the Camino Real, such a sophisticated and sturdy vehicle would have been necessary to withstand the hardships of the trail.

The Mexican carreta was of the same fundamental design as that used for more than three thousand years by peoples of Asia Minor and southern Europe. In 1958, Soviet archaeologists uncovered several intact carts between the Caspian and Black seas, dating from about 1400 B.C., whose three-part disc wheels and axle arrangement bore a striking similarity to New Mexican carretas. From Roman times down to the present day, carts in Spain have been made according to the traditional pattern, although variations in wheel type and body form, representing the whims of individual cartwrights, have brought about superficial stylistic differences in some regions.

The first carreta built in the Viceroyalty of New Spain, indeed, in the New World, was the handiwork of Sebastián de Aparicio who began transporting freight over the Camino Real between Veracruz and Mexico City in 1536. After that year, the manufacture of carts expanded rapidly. In the last decade of the century, Juan de Oñate included a number of carretas among the vehicles making up his supply train bound from Zacatecas to colonize the upper Rio Grande valley.

In the decades before the Pueblo Revolt, it appears that several professional cartwrights settled in New Mexico and helped launch local production of carretas. Pueblo Indian labor was sometimes used in the manufacturing process. In 1660, ten new carretas were reportedly made for the governor who used them to ship

83

assorted merchandise to the settlements in Nueva Vizcaya. We can assume that these carts were built with considerable precision and strength, since they were destined for commerce on the Camino Real.

Colonial records occasionally mention citizens whose occupation is listed as carreta maker. Unfortunately the information is too thin in most cases to determine whether this represented specialized, full-time employment or whether, as seems more likely, cartwrighting was merely an adjunct of general carpentry.

While it is possible to ascertain from a study of existing carretas the standard design and method of construction, nevertheless, many procedures and customs associated with the craft remain a mystery. No colonial cartwright, as far as we know, kept a journal noting the qualities he looked for in selecting proper wood for his task or outlining the steps in fabricating a cart from start to finish.

Capt. Henry Smith Turner, an officer with Gen. Stephen W. Kearny's Army of the West, provides an illuminating comment about carretas. In his diary of 1846, Turner recalled that, while traveling along the Rio Grande below Albuquerque, "We occasionally see a grove of cottonwood which is preserved with great care, as it furnishes the only material with which carts for the whole country are made. These groves are always private property." His statement lends weight to the conclusion that carreta making was an important cottage industry in Hispanic New Mexico.

Muleteering

⚜

A *rrieros somos y algun dia en el camino nos encontramos.*
"Mule drovers are we and some day on the trail
we shall meet." Here is the traditional refrain spoken
by packtrain men upon parting throughout Mexico and
our own Southwest. This simple phrase, perhaps better
than any other, symbolizes the life and spirit of the old
arrieros who have now all but vanished.

Arriería was the highly respected and useful profes-
sion of packing mules, burros, and occasionally horses.
The *arriero* or packer formed part of an occupational
group whose members were bound together in what
almost amounted to a brotherhood. The difficult skills
involved in packing and transporting goods, the inti-
mate knowledge of animal care and behavior, and the
hardships of life on desert and mountain trails all worked

to cement strong bonds of loyalty and comradeship among *arrieros* and to set them off as a breed apart.

Sons followed their fathers, learning from them both the techniques a muleteer needed in handling a *recua* or packtrain and the rigorous code which demanded honesty and hardihood above all else. George W. Kendall, a New Orleans newsman, described New Mexican *arrieros* he encountered, in the early 1840s, as men whose "word may invariably be depended upon and who look to the interest of those who employ them with scrupulous care, taking every precaution to guard the goods entrusted to their charge from being stolen or damaged, and despising lying and deceit." Bearing out this extravagant praise were many instances of mine owners of northern Mexico who placed entire fortunes in gold and silver bullion in the hands of *arrieros* for shipment, and so far as history and tradition record, never had their confidence misplaced.

The management of a packtrain, whether it carried treasure or simple domestic goods, was a serious and complicated business. The overseer or *mayordomo* of a large train held responsibility for the safety and well-being of his men and animals, selected the trail routes and campsites, and set the number of hours of travel per day. He could usually be identified by his flashy appearance, fine trailwise horse upon which he was mounted, and silver embellishments on his saddle gear.

The *mayordomo*'s assistant was the *cargador* (head packer) who supervised the loading and unloading of the mules by the *arrieros*. The packer's day began with the first light of dawn when the mules were driven in from the grazing ground. A bellmare served to keep the herd together at night and to lead the train on the day's

86

Arrieros packing a blindfolded mule in the traditional way. (From State Historical Society of Colorado, photo no. F-14690)

march. In turn, the animals were roped out and led to the *arrieros* who worked in pairs at loading up. The first step was to render the mule docile so that packing could proceed in an orderly manner. This was usually accomplished by use of the *tapojos* or blindfold. Ordinarily these were simple leather blinds with a strap that fastened behind the ears. Sometimes, however, proud owners provided *tapojos* of wool or even silk which carried fancy embroidery in gold thread and the mule's name in stitching.

The first article to be placed on the animal's back

was a square saddle cloth called a *jerga*. Upon this rested either a sheepskin or leather pocket-pads stuffed with grass. On the padding a packsaddle could be set and secured by a broad grass cinch which was pulled tight amidst groans and wheezes, until it appeared the long-eared creature would be cut in two. Here, of course, lay the secret of secure packing. A short distance up the trail, the saddle fastenings would have loosened enough so the mule could breathe comfortably, but the straps remained sufficiently tight so he would not gall or become sore-backed.

The two *arrieros* were now ready for the pack. If the load consisted of a single bundle, the *arrieros* placed it on top, if two, they balanced it on either side of the saddle. A straw mat, the *petate,* functioned as a cover and the whole load was firmly tied down with a lash rope and cinch. The *arrieros* hauled on their slack with a knee braced against the animal's side until the rope was taut. Then one would shout ¡*Adios!* and his companion would respond ¡*Vaya!* (Get along there!); they would slap the mule on the rump and send him trotting away to join his brethren who had already received their burdens and were snatching a few last mouthfuls of breakfast.

So skilled were the *arrieros* at their trade that a mule could be readied in the manner just described in the space of three to five minutes. Such speed and dexterity were necessary when a train numbered several hundred pack animals. These longer *recuas* were often divided into segments, known as *atajos* or strings, and were spaced at intervals under the *mayordomo*'s direction to facilitate handling.

When night camp was made, unloading proceeded

in a manner precisely opposite from that of the previous morning. Considerable care was taken to arrange the packsaddles and packs in regular order so that each mule could receive his same gear and load on the following day. Then all the equipment was covered with the *petates* to protect it from any sudden rain storm.

Once the animals had been attended and turned out with their mare, the *arrieros* looked to their own comfort. One mule always served as the commissary department and carried, in addition to foodstuffs, a *metate* or grinding stone upon which corn was reduced to fresh meal for *tortillas*. The office of cook was undertaken in turn by each of the *arrieros,* and after their sparse evening meal, they sat about the campfire smoking corn husk cigarettes and swapping tales of other journeys or of some particularly memorable mule.

The methods and lore of *arriería* or muleteering have their roots far back in Spanish history. The Spaniards of the Middle Ages were horsemen par excellence, and because of the rugged terrain of the Iberian Peninsula were greatly dependent upon the use of packtrains for transport. A good deal of their knowledge concerning horse and mule culture derived from the Arabs and Moors of North Africa who occupied Spain from the eighth to the fifteenth centuries.

The Arabs were a nation of cavalry and mule or camel packers and much of what they knew they introduced to the Spaniards. This is reflected most clearly today in the Spanish language which retains mostly Arabic names for horse colors. And Arabic terms fill the mule packer's vocabulary. The very name *arriería* derives from Arabic *arre,* meaning "get along" as addressed to burros and mules. According to tradition, Queen Isabella, who personally led her army in the final defeat of the Islamic invaders, was supplied by a train of fifteen thousand packmules.

Wherever the Spaniards undertook discovery and conquest in the New World, they went well-mounted and with pack animals in tow. The island of Jamaica early became a breeding ground for horses, mules, and donkeys and the source of supply for adventurers who launched expeditions to the mainland. Soon after the conquest of Mexico, *arrieros* could be found leading their laden packtrains into the farthest recesses of the country.

Mules very quickly overshadowed horses in popularity and were widely employed not only as pack animals but as saddle mules and draft teams for the carriages of the wealthy classes. In fact, the municipal council of Mexico City became so alarmed at the lack of interest in horse raising that it issued a law requiring all citizens to use and maintain the same number of horses as mules.

From Mexico City huge packtrains, numbering hundreds of animals and scores of *arrieros*, strung out on the trails leading northward to the remote Spanish provinces of Texas, New Mexico, and California. These packtrains bore all the assorted goods needed to sustain the missions and military garrisons on the northern frontier. In later colonial times, the men with their mules and burros converged each year on the town of San Juan del Rio, north of the capital, to attend a great trading fair where products from the frontier were exchanged for manufactured merchandise. Here the *arrieros*, who according to one source sometimes brought together 50,000 pack animals, indulged themselves in gambling, wild dances, and frolics with the local belles.

Arrieros remained a common fixture of rural Mexican life until the coming of the railroad in the late nineteenth century. Today some vestiges of *arriería* still survive in mountainous and isolated sections of central and southern Mexico. Mule and burro packing, on the Mexican mold, persisted in our own Southwest until fairly recently; and as late as the 1940s burro trains laden with firewood could still be seen on the streets of Santa Fe.

The *arriero*, however, like the blacksmith and the wheelwright belongs to another era. Even those persons who presently employ packtrains in our national forests and wilderness areas cannot capture the true spirit or feeling of the old muleteer. His was a life of eternal hardship with few of the amenities of civilized life to ease his long journeys. His indomitable spirit and devotion to his duties can be seen in another of the many proverbs common to the men of the trail: "Better to be an *arriero* than to be rich."

The Lore of Sheep
and Goats

✥

I n his wise and observant little book, *Tongues of the Monte, The Mexico I Like*, J. Frank Dobie included a chapter entitled, "The Man of Goats." In it he describes the life of a simple goat herder he visited several miles south of the border. "Such herders, commonly regarded as ignorant, make much better company than scholarly Doctors of Philosophy," declared Dobie.

By that statement, the author not only expressed his aversion for stuffy professors, he suggested that native tenders of animals have something to say to those willing to listen. Living close to the land, following a lonely occupation, and dependent largely on their own resources, herders of goats and herders of sheep possessed a fascinating body of knowledge regarding their way of life.

No one yet has gathered together the lore of Southwestern herders and told their story, as it should be told. Dobie could have done it since he had a knack for that sort of thing. But other subjects in the folklore line engaged his attention, so he passed this one by.

In New Mexico, where sheep-raising was once the predominant industry, only a few Hispanos are left who go off with their flocks to summer ranges in the northern mountains. Several I have met retain some faint recollection of the traditions common a century ago. But mostly, the hard life and tricks of the trade known by colonial herders have been forgotten.

Many of the details, however, have been preserved in scattered accounts by early travelers, government reports on economic life, and even in folk tales and legends recorded in the early part of this century. Some writer, with the nose of a detective, could assemble all that material and come away with a bang-up book.

His narrative would necessarily begin with the Spaniards Coronado and Oñate, bringers of the first sheep and goats to the Southwest in the sixteenth century. In the years that followed, the flocks of sheep expanded enormously in spite of constant raids by the Indians. In the 1780s, one Navajo is supposed to have said that his warriors were careful never to steal all the sheep from any one hacienda on the Rio Grande. They didn't want to put the rancher out of business, otherwise they would have nothing to steal on the next year's raid.

Those Spanish flocks of sheep always had some goats mixed in with them. They made excellent leaders. When the herder wanted to corral his flock, he yelled at the goats who promptly took the lead with the sheep following. The goat was smart, not only in this respect,

93

A man on a burro tends his herd of goats. (From El Paso Public Library)

but he remained alert always on the lookout for coyotes and danger.

The goats had other uses, too. A single black one was buddied up to each 100 sheep. These blacks were called *marcaderos* (markers). A herder could cast his eye across several thousand animals and by counting the markers be reasonably certain that no part of the flock was missing.

Nanny goats also made good mothers for orphan lambs, or what sheepmen today call bum lambs. The nanny, without much persuasion, would nurse the orphan along with one or two of her own kids. Of course, the mother goats supplied milk, too, for the herders whose diet was both skimpy and simple.

Many *pastores*, or herders, were wholly lacking in education. So, they could not count beyond the number of fingers on both hands. This was a serious disadvantage when it came to selling some of their own animals. The purchaser had to buy and pay for one sheep at a time because of the seller's inability to reckon the total.

The herder had a problem as well in tallying the flock for his *patrón*, the owner. He could count up to 10 using his fingers, and upon reaching that number he added a white stone to a pile and began counting again. When the *patrón* appeared and asked for a tally, his man handed him a sack of stones.

Some herders went a bit further. They used a black stone to represent 10 white stones, which meant 100 sheep. The *patrón* must have been grateful for even this small improvement in counting.

Every animal that was lost to wolves, lightning, rattlesnake bite or other mishap was charged to the poor herder, who had to make it good from his paltry wage. Dead sheep were skinned, ears and all, and the pelt was kept and shown to the *patrón* so he would know how it had died.

The early breeds of Spanish sheep and goats have just about disappeared. But some 400 examples of a colonial type of sheep with 4 horns have recently been counted on the Navajo Reservation. The Indians like its long fleece and use it in the weaving of their famous rugs.

Some ranchers in the Chama Valley are trying to save the breed, which they call Navajosa. The wool, after being cleaned and spun, brings $15 a pound. These sheep, to my mind, are even more valuable as a rare historical survival.

New Mexican Ciboleros
on the Buffalo Plains

✠

Handsome, young Manuel Maes, so the old *corrido* or New Mexican folksong goes, came to a tragic end while engaged in his favorite occupation. Manuel was a *cibolero*, a New Mexican buffalo hunter. In 1863 he joined with a hunting party going to the Llano Estacado, the high plains of eastern New Mexico and western Texas.

Near present day Amarillo, the *ciboleros* spotted a herd of the large, shaggy animals and gave chase. Like his companions, Manuel was armed, not with a rifle, but with a steel-tipped lance. The New Mexicans, on superbly trained horses, were accustomed to dashing up alongside the fleeing buffalo and delivering a mortal wound with a swift jab of the lance. The maneuver required dexterity and courage. These the *ciboleros* had developed to a high degree.

From the swirl of dust, an excited Manuel selected a fat cow and spurred his horse in for the kill. But suddenly his mount shied and Manuel lost his balance. The lance spun about, was struck by the surging mass of buffaloes, and the point was driven deep into the young man's body. Racing up, the other hunters found him crumpled in a bloody heap on the prairie grass.

Manuel Maes was left in an unmarked grave on the Llano Estacado. But his memory, and that of others who over the years perished in the chase, froze to death, or became forever lost on the trackless plains, was preserved in ballad and folk tale.

By any standard of measurement, the *ciboleros* and their way of life were extraordinarily picturesque. The men dressed in homemade leather shirts and short leather pants that just covered the knees. They were shod with *teguas*, the hard-soled hide moccasins characteristic of the New Mexican settlements. And on their heads they wore a curious pointed hat of leather adorned with a gracefully curving feather. Such bonnets would perhaps seem to you and me more appropriate for Robin Hood and his merry band. Yet for a hundred years or more, they were the reigning fashion among hunters on the southern plains.

Lances, like the one that took the life of the unfortunate Manuel Maes, possessed a shaft six to eight feet long. The broad, double-edged point, forged from an old plowshare or worn out rasp, averaged twelve to sixteen inches in length. A number of these old *cibolero* lances can be seen in collections of the Museum of New Mexico at Santa Fe and in the Kit Carson Museum at Taos. Farmers in the Española Valley occasionally turn one up when they are cleaning their irrigation ditches.

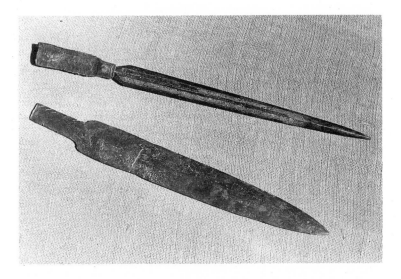

Steel lance points of the *ciboleros* are occasionally found on the Plains today. (From the collection of Marc Simmons)

Buffalo hunting was long an important part of New Mexico's economy. After the fall harvest each year, people up and down the Rio Grande and the Pecos began planning expeditions to the plains. Several villages often banded together to send a large train of hunters and ox carts to secure the winter's meat supply.

A favorite rendezvous for Spanish settlers in the Mora region was the village of Lucero, nicknamed La Placita de los Ciboleros. In late September, those wishing to go on the hunt met at Lucero with lances, skinning knives, and carts. On the eve of their departure, the townsfolk gave a farewell dance so the hunters and their helpers could have a frolic before undertaking the hardships and loneliness of prairie travel.

From Lucero and Taos, from Santa Cruz and Santa Fe, San Miguel del Vado and Manzano, and even from far away El Paso hunting caravans rumbled onto the Llano Estacado. When a herd was met after weeks on the trail, the mayordomo of the company selected a campsite near a water hole and ordered his people to prepare for the chase on the following day.

At dawn the lancers took their swiftest horses and went in pursuit of the buffalo. As soon as they had downed one, they immediately went on to the next, leaving their helpers, *los siguidores*, to come behind and slit the animal's throat to be sure it was dead. Finally, the carts arrived with the butchers who cut up the carcasses and hauled them back to camp.

For days everyone worked feverishly salting down the hides, rendering tallow, and converting fresh meat into *tasajo* or jerky. Each caravan carried a good supply of fiber rope which could be stretched between carts or from poles to form drying lines. As the meat was cut into long thin strips, it was draped over these lines and then left to the sun and the air. When thoroughly dry, the "jerked" meat was packed in bags for the journey back to the settlements.

Besides the hides and jerky, the men often took home a supply of marrow bones favored by their wives for making stew. The tongues of the buffalo they carefully preserved by salting, for these could be sent south to the markets of Chihuahua where they fetched a peso apiece. The buffalo tallow was especially prized for greasing the wheels of the carts and for soap and candle

100

making. New Mexican candles were an important item of export and they went to light homes, mines and altars all over northern Mexico.

Once the hunting and processing were completed, the cart trains started homeward. The men were usually in a rollicky mood, knowing that their families would have meat for the winter table and that a little profit would be left from the sale of hides and tongues. As the season was far gone, they might be forced to march against a driven snow or to sleep nights with a furious wind tugging at their blankets. Such discomforts seldom dampened their high spirits, and they were in the habit of jogging along and singing in chorus. The songs, composed on the spur of the moment, told of their own adventures or those of some renowned *cibolero*, such as Manuel Maes. Altogether the color and pageantry of a buffalo hunter caravan on the move presented a picture that a later-day Hollywood film maker might have envied.

Traveling to or from the plains, one danger constantly at the elbow of every *cibolero* was that posed by hostile Indians. The problem was so acute in 1830 that the governor in Santa Fe sent 25 soldiers and a cannon to accompany hunters from San Miguel del Vado. The fall buffalo harvest, the governor believed, was far too important for New Mexico to allow any disruption.

Most years, however, the *ciboleros* depended upon their own arms and courage for defense. If a war party appeared on the horizon, they circled their ox carts, much as the Anglo pioneers drew up their covered wagons for defense. In spite of the danger, the New Mexicans returned to their familiar haunts on the plains, time after time. Soon their creaking cart wheels formed well-worn trails leading from the Hondo Valley near modern Roswell, eastward over the Mescalero Ridge, and from the upper Rio Grande valley out to such well-known landmarks as Tucumcari Mountain and the Rabbit Ears near Clayton.

The *ciboleros* and their way of life have long since vanished from New Mexico's eastern plains, but a faint echo of their passing can still be found in a few folk tales and ballads and in an occasional footnote in the history books.

Nobility in Mexico

⚜

In spite of a long tradition of egalitarianism, the western world still tends to look with awe upon a noble title. Members of old European aristocracy, though exiled and impoverished, seem to wear a romantic mantle. They are much in demand at formal dinners and cocktail parties. An American woman is deemed fortunate when she weds a ruling prince, as Grace Kelly managed to do, or for that matter, even an aging Russian count with holes in his shoes.

In colonial times, Spaniards too had a passion for titles, perhaps even more so than the nobility-struck Englishmen. Many Spanish families first gained noble rank during the medieval wars with the Moors as a reward for extraordinary military service. In the twelfth century, for example, two brothers named López led an assault on the Moorish-held Portuguese city of Chaves and captured it. A grateful king made them knights and ordered that their name should, thereafter, be López de Chaves. The brothers' descendants long afterward helped explore the New World, and the name Chaves (or Chavez) is a common one now in northern Mexico.

Practically every Spanish commoner hoped someday to advance at least to the lowest noble rank, that of hidalgo. The term ostensibly comes from the contraction of three words, *hijo de algo*, meaning simply, "son of something." Those who could accumulate enough wealth were able to buy the title from the king. But most poor people had to count on winning it through some valued deed.

The position had its concrete benefits. Hidalgos were exempt from taxes, and they couldn't be arrested for debt, like the common folk. And they could pass on the title to a male heir. Among status-conscious Spaniards, hidalgo rank was much coveted. Historian Jaime Vicens Vives tells us that for long Spain was infected with hidalgo-mania. A man might be poor as a church mouse, but he wanted that title. An old Spanish joke defines a hidalgo as a man who hasn't eaten for three days, but appears on the street chewing on a toothpick, as if he'd just finished a banquet. The hidalgo had pride, even if his pantry was bare. Appearances were everything.

When the conquistador Juan de Oñate was preparing to march north in the closing years of the sixteenth century, he ran into trouble enlisting colonists. Spaniards well knew the dangers and hardships they would find in the northern deserts and were not eager to sign on. The king lent a hand by proclaiming that every man who joined Oñate and stuck with the settlement in the

Aristocratic New Mexican don. (From Andrew K. Gregg, *New Mexico in the Nineteenth Century* [1968])

north for five years would be made a hidalgo. Recruitment speeded up after that.

Most of the leaders of the expeditions to the harsh northern frontiers were given lofty titles. Governor Diego de Vargas, who reconquered the vast territory of New Mexico after the Pueblo Revolt, was a marqués.

Noblemen invariably added the title *don* before their first name, as Don José or Don Manuel. The usual explanation is that the term *don* comes from combining the first letters in the phrase *de origen noble*. However, Fay Blake of Albuquerque, a scholar of Jewish history, maintains that the word derives from the Hebrew *adonas*, which means *Our Lord*.

A curious use of the title *don* occurred in colonial days. Priests sent by the Bishop of Durango to serve on the Rio Grande alongside the Franciscan missionaries were addressed as *don* instead of Father, even though they had no claim to nobility.

After Mexico became independent from Spain and formal titles of nobility were abandoned, the term *don* continued to be used willy-nilly for any man of wealth or who had reached an advanced age. Even today it is common to address someone as *don*, merely as a mark of respect and esteem. It is a charming custom, one that has its roots deep in the colonial past of New Mexico.

Part Two

Wills as History

❖

O ne of the most interesting and valuable class of
documents from the Spanish colonial period in the
Southwest is the will. Since the early Spaniards left us
few personal letters and diaries, these wills help fill the
gap by revealing details of daily life and custom.

Under Spanish law there were two types of papers
dealing with the inheritance of an estate. The first was
the will itself, called the *testamento,* prepared by the individual before death. The second was the *hijuela* con-
sisting of the inventory of the estate made by government
officials after death occurred. Hundreds of these documents remain in our archives, available for study.

Among Spanish settlers a will was a statement of
piety as much as it was a dispersal of the estate. Provision was usually made for bequests to the church,
special masses and prayers, the wake, and in the cases

of important persons, burial inside the church. The will also specified the sum to be paid to the priest for the funeral. One prominent rancher who died on the Rio Grande in 1812 included these charitable bequests in his will: money to prisoners in the local jail; money to bashful women and maidens, to be chosen by the priest; and money to unfortunate persons, also to be chosen by the priest.

The size of the estate and the value of each item listed in the *hijuela*, or inventory, give a good picture of prevailing economic conditions. The variety of personal belongings, such as household goods, farm and ranch equipment, livestock, and weapons serve both as a barometer of wealth and a measure of a person's social standing in the community.

One of the earliest wills we have was dictated by a leading figure of the colonial years, Gov. Diego de Vargas. In 1704 while campaigning against the Apaches, he fell seriously ill. Taken by his soldiers to the nearest town, Bernalillo, he barely had time to make his will before he died.

Included were instructions that his body be carried to Santa Fe and given an elaborate funeral with much pomp and splendor. Then he was to be buried under the altar of the main church. The governor also instructed that on the day of these ceremonies his estate should pay for 50 bushels of corn and 12 head of cattle to be distributed to the poor. Such generosity was common to the nobility and Vargas held the title of marquis.

To his children and his friends the governor left a large sum of money and many expensive possessions. Among the latter were silver vessels, a pair of pearl earrings with emeralds, diamond rings, fancy clothes of

Don Diego de Vargas's feeble signature as el Marques de la Naba de Brazubas on his last will a day before his death in April 1704. (From John L. Kessell, et al., *Remote Beyond Compare* [1989]) brocade and silk, saddles, sets of pistols, decorated swords, and his favorite gold cane. These and similar articles show that while Vargas lived on a raw frontier in an adobe palace, he was able to surround himself with symbols of wealth.

The will of a more humble citizen, Elena Gallegos, provides a useful contrast. She was a poor widow residing in Albuquerque when she composed her will in 1731. Elena had lived in the area before the Pueblo Revolt of 1680. During that terrible uprising she had fled south to El Paso with her husband and son. During the period of exile, her spouse died. So when the reconquest of upper New Mexico was completed in 1693 she returned north with her uncle.

At her death Elena owned a large piece of land with a residence on it. She also listed livestock to the number of 32 head of cattle, 2 yoke of oxen, 12 mares, and 2 mules. For the rest there were a couple of silk petticoats, a shawl, a cloak, some corral bracelets, and a few other trinkets.

The curious thing is that the lady described herself as living in poverty. While her personal articles were, indeed, meager, the size of her land holdings and livestock scarcely suggest a person in want. But then maybe all of her neighbors owned a good deal more and she felt deprived.

Incidentally, the Elena Gallegos land grant on the east side of Albuquerque is today worth millions of dollars, something that its original owner could never have imagined.

A remarkable fact is that these old Spanish wills were almost never contested by the heirs. The reason seems to have been that the wishes of the dying were held in great respect, even reverence. That should remind us that even when life was comfortless and primitive, as it was in colonial New Mexico, noble sentiments could still flourish.

Reading History

❖

T he three Spanish colonial documents, translated and printed in this section, furnish a capsule view of economic and social conditions in New Mexico during the late eighteenth and early nineteenth centuries. They are examples of primary sources, or in other words, original written records that historians can use in the collecting and verifying of evidence about the past.

The value of every historical document depends upon its accuracy and completeness of observation. Unhappily, faithful testimony is not the rule, since human beings are prone to falsify their statements, either deliberately or unconsciously. When to this impediment is added the fact that for any past event or period only a limited quantity of evidence is ever available, it will be seen how difficult it is for the historian to speak with confidence.

The good scholar takes these limitations into account, along with other variables and his own tendency to make subjective judgments. Then he attempts to reconstruct the past, knowing full well that his conclusions must remain tentative. Historians exist at the mercy of their sources, so that when new documents surface, old views and interpretations may have to be quickly jettisoned.

It has been commonly observed that historians work like detectives. They search out clues, assemble and weigh fragmentary evidence, try to solve mysteries, and explain to others what actually happened in times gone by. The challenges presented by these activities are perhaps what make the study of history such an engaging and stimulating pursuit.

The three New Mexican documents presented here illustrate both the usefulness of this kind of historical material and the problems associated with their proper interpretation. Two of the reports are by governors, each of whom served eleven-year terms at Santa Fe—Pedro Fermín de Mendinueta (1767–1778) and Fernando de Chacón (1794–1805). Both men were born in Spain and had a long record of distinguished military service before receiving their appointments by the crown to the governorship of New Mexico. Understandably, they tended to view provincial affairs from the perspective of an outsider, one whose sympathy lay not with the home folk but rather with the needs of the Spanish Empire and the desires of His Majesty. That circumstance, however, probably lent their words a degree of objectivity that would have been absent had they been native-born members of frontier society.

The third report, which chronologically falls between the governors' two accounts, was written by an industrious and scholarly Franciscan, Fray Juan Agustín de Morfí, in 1778. His pointed observations on conditions in New Mexico seem to have been drawn, not from his own personal experience, but rather from first hand information supplied him by fellow Franciscans on the scene, most notably the much-travelled Fray Silvestre Vélez de Escalante. As most readers of Spanish American history are well aware, colonial missionaries developed a view of public affairs that was colored by their religious calling and mind set. Thus, Father Morfí speaks in laudatory fashion of the Pueblo Indians' social practices and work habits, which by inference the Franciscans might claim some credit in developing.

Governor Mendinueta also praises the Pueblos but seems to suggest that their superior qualities are a gift of nature, although nourished by contact with Spanish institutions in general. He specifically criticizes the missionaries for their shortage of personnel and for an unwillingness or inability to learn the several Pueblo languages. By comparing and contrasting the words of Father Morfí and Governor Mendinueta, we are led that much closer to comprehending a fragment of the true history of New Mexico in the 1770s.

It has become popular recently in many academic circles to deny the possibility of objectivity in dealing with any written historical sources. With reference to Spaniards, some scholars have gone so far as to state that they were so constricted by their own cultural and religious standpoints they could only write propaganda, whether consciously or unconsciously. They recorded not what they saw, but what they wished to see.

Researchers who have read widely in the Spanish

archival record must recognize the falsity of such a sweeping generalization. Spaniards, like other people, borrowed both from reality and illusion in producing a record of their activity. It is up to the modern-day reader to exercise caution and skepticism in sorting out which is which. Indeed, the work of separating fact from fiction, honing as it does an individual's analytic skills, provides one of the chief benefits of historical inquiry.

Indian and Mission Affairs
in 1773

G overnor Pedro Fermín de Mendinueta, who served at
Santa Fe from 1767 to 1778, was an iron-fisted
military man with a reputation for settling Indian
disturbances the hard way. During his lengthy
administration, hostile Apaches and Comanches assailed
New Mexico from all sides, keeping him and his soldiers
constantly in the field. While the governor won some
notable victories, he was unable to achieve a lasting peace,
owing to a scarcity of resources and to the province's poor
defenses.

   After assessing the troublesome situation, Mendinueta
wrote the viceroy in Mexico City, enclosing two
recommendations. The first urged the issuance of a royal
order that would compel the citizens of New Mexico to
forsake their scattered farms and move into small but
compact walled-towns that could be easily defended. The

118

second urged the royal government to loosen its purse strings and fund the placing of a new military presidio at Taos, to back up the only other garrison in the province, the one at Santa Fe.

Mendinueta got his decree, ordering the populace to concentrate in fortified settlements, but it proved very difficult to enforce. On the other matter, he could get nowhere at all—his request for a Taos presidio was quietly shelved and forgotten. His lack of success, in part, had to do with the attitude of the viceroy, Antonio Bucareli y Ursua. As a man of natural piety and charity, the viceroy wished to settle the problem of hostile Indians on the frontier through peaceful rather than military means.

Unhappily, the futility of trying to win over the Indians by resort to missionary activity had been demonstrated on many occasions during the previous century. But still Bucareli persevered. On September 2, 1772, he addressed a general letter to governors on the northern frontier, including Mendinueta, asking for an honest assessment of Indian affairs and the status of the mission program in their respective provinces. At the same time, he appealed to the heads of the several religious orders headquartered in the viceregal capital with a request to have knowledgeable friars who had served on the frontier furnish the government a written statement of their own views and recommendations.

Of the responses Bucareli received from civil officials and churchmen, the report composed by Governor Mendinueta of New Mexico proved to be one of the most interesting. It contained blunt comments on the government and economy of his province and clearly expressed his belief on the hopelessness of endeavoring to gain the allegiance of

119

the nomadic tribes through peaceful persuasion or religious conversion.

It was Mendinueta's first hand experience as a military campaigner on New Mexico's beleaguered frontier that caused him to put little faith in ecclesiastical efforts to convert the enemy. His scepticism in this regard is clearly evident in the "Report of Missions" he submitted in 1773 and which follows here.* That the document had much influence on the subsequent formation of Spain's Indian policy is doubtful. Nevertheless, Mendinueta's remarks retain historical value because of the brief glimpse they give of a distant and vanished society.

THE REPORT

Dear Sir: Your Excellency orders me in a letter of last September 2nd, which included an authorized copy of the opinion of the Fiscal, to prepare a report according to what my experience dictates regarding the improvement of the temporal and spiritual welfare of the missions within my governmental jurisdiction, and the reduction of the infidels who surround it. And to fulfill accurately my obligation it seemed appropriate to me to set forth the state of the missions and the temporal and spiritual government which has been practiced in them up until the present, and it is as follows:

From the time of the reconquest of this province (which was in the last years of the past century), the

---

*The translation was made from a copy of the document in the Archivo General de la Nación, Mexico, Provincias Internas, vol. 152.

native Indians have always lived in a civilized manner. Reduced to twenty-one pueblos which are formed on plazas or streets with houses of two and three stories, the individuals of each one of these pueblos annually elect a governor (*gobernadorcillo*), a war captain (*capitán mayor de la guerra*), and some other subordinate officers. All proceed to the governor of the province who confirms them in their offices and who makes known to them their duties which under oath they promise to fulfill.

In every two, three, or more pueblos the governor names an *alcalde mayor* who serves the Indians as well as the Spanish citizens of that district, with the aid of one or more *tenientes* according to the number of pueblos and settlements of Spaniards. This is done in order that all may easily have recourse to the law when cases arise. But with this difference, the Indians are not charged fees under any circumstances. And the aforementioned *alcaldes mayores* and *tenientes*, in addition to fulfilling their official duties with care and punishing common wrongdoers with the moderation befitting these neophytes, are obliged to go out with the Indians of their respective pueblos on campaigns which occur frequently.

Agriculture comes so natural to these Indians that their pueblos are the storehouses of all kinds of grain (especially corn). Thither come the Spanish citizens to make purchases, as well as the governor when grain is needed by the presidial paymaster for the troops. Prices are those uniformly established throughout the province. They succeed well with their cattle and sheep and with their few horses. All benefit from this except those most exposed on the frontier who suffer continually from the enemy. They weave *mantas* of wool and cotton for their simple clothing. And finally, they are obedient and quick to act whenever orders are given them which serve the interest of the King. These are carried out with a delight and attention to detail which have become well known.

At the base of political government previously referred to are found these prosperous pueblos well supplied with all the necessities of life and exhibiting not the slightest trace of unfaithfulness. As a result of this, the briefness of my report should be expected, I having set forth without addition or omission the established form of government.

Visible spiritual government is by the Reverend Father Missionaries who are the friars of the regular Order of St. Francis of the Province of the Holy Gospel. They select from the mission Indians the sacristans and *fiscales*, the former to serve them at Mass and care for the sacristy, and the latter to call together every day the *doctrineros* (as those who are not married are called) to say prayers, the Commandments, the Articles, and to partake of the Sacraments.[1] And everyone is summoned on holy days to hear Mass and to recite all that I just mentioned, and this is always done in a loud voice following the lead of the *fiscal*.

The aforementioned missionaries administer the Holy Sacraments of baptism, extreme unction, and marriage to the Indians on all occasions, but that of penitence, as a rule, only on the point of death and then by means of an interpreter. I am convinced that the reason for this is that the friars do not know the language of the Indians, and these cannot understand Castillian well, notwithstanding that a superior order has been proclaimed to correct this situation.[2]

A traditional New Mexico village, here depicted in the 1880s, would have looked quite similar in the colonial period. (From the collection of Marc Simmons)

Although following the voice of the *fiscal*, as I said above, all seem to know what they are saying by memory, on being separated from that voice and called upon individually, those are rare who can do anything, and even rarer are those who understand the Mysteries they recite. In the latter cases comprehension seems to come by chance since it occurs so infrequently. Regarding such an important matter, it seems to me it would be advantageous for Your Excellency to convey some of your religious zeal to the superior prelates so that Your Excellency's desire for the success of Catholicism and the pious wishes of Our Sovereign may be realized.

I feel compelled to inform Your Excellency that for the administration of the twenty-one Indian pueblos of this province, and that of St. Thomas of Abiquíu composed of *genízaro* Indians[3] established in the time of my predecessor Don Tomás Vélez Cachupín, and the three *villas*[4] within this government, there is not at the present more than sixteen friars. To confirm what I am saying, the pueblo of Nuestra Señora de Guadalupe de Zuñi which comprises more than 1500 souls and which is thirty leagues distant from Acoma, the nearest point, has been for many years without the services of a missionary although in the past it was the practice to have two (which I deem necessary considering the number of people). I dispatched my official letter on this point to the Reverend Father Custodian of these missions, and also on this matter I informed His Excellency the Viceroy Marqués de Croix in a letter dated April 29 of the year sixty-nine. By virtue of this and an official opinion of the *asesor-general*,[5] His Excellency was pleased to order me to inform him of certain points concerning this affair which I did in a letter of July 30, 1770. Nevertheless, the same lack of missionaries continues as I described it in the above-mentioned pueblo, and the only thing that takes place is that a friar goes once a year to baptize and marry. I leave to the Christian understanding of Your Excellency the task of imagining the state of spiritual abandonment among those neophytes. My own careless understanding finds itself afflicted with the liveliest pain.

Regarding the reduction of the pagan Indians, no little effort has been expended by both the governors and the friars. Because of this, there were formed about twenty years ago two missions among the Navajo Indians. But these proved a failure within a few days since the Indians who had congregated retired to the mountains and left the missionaries alone. There is no hope

of attracting the Navajos back to the tranquil magnif-
icence of our Catholic religion on account of their natural
wild disposition which differs little from the fierce beasts.

For this same reason it has not been possible to
reduce some Apaches called Jicarillas who, despoiled of
their lands by the Comanches, have been living for many
years in this region in huts of their own making near
the pueblos of Pecos and Taos. Although they have been
offered on several occasions lands to work where they
might form their own pueblos, neither this nor seeing
the practical and comfortable life enjoyed by the Christian Indians, nor the miseries which they themselves
suffer is sufficient to diminish their brutal inclination.
And if with these, who are the ones among whom less
obstacles are encountered and who would benefit the
greatest by submitting, no progress can be made in con-
gregating them, then how much less hope remains for
the Comanches, Utes, Faraon and Gila Apaches, unless
God Our Father, being all powerful and infinitely mer-
ciful, enlightens their understanding.

What has been related to this point is all that can
be touched on in a brief treatment of the present subject
for Your Excellency. I am convinced it will be sufficient
for your insight and penetrating reason to form a judg-
ment which as always will be the best possible.

I pray that God in His greatness will see fit to guard
Your Excellency many years.

Santa Fé, New Mexico, 8 of January, 1773.

Your most reverent and obedient servant kisses
the hands of your Excellency.

Pedro Fermín de Mendinueta:

To the Most Excellent Viceroy
Don Antonio Bucareli y Ursua.

NOTES TO THE REPORT

1. The word *doctrinero* usually referred to friars who were giving religious instruction to Indians.

2. The order mentioned here by the Governor was issued by the Bishop of Durango in 1760. After a visit to New Mexico in which he noted the inability of the friars to speak the native tongue, the Bishop commanded them to engage in the study of Indian languages so that interpreters might be dispensed with, especially in the preaching of sermons and the hearing of confessions.

3. *Genízaro* was a generic term applied to nomadic Indians who were captured by the Spaniards or purchased by them from the plains tribes and who were educated as Christians. Initially the *genízaros* acted as servants of the Spanish citizens, but because of ill-treatment they petitioned the government for permission to form their own towns on the frontiers of New Mexico. One of the earliest of their settlements was at Abiquiu and the patron was St. Thomas.

4. The three *villas* were Santa Fe, Albuquerque, and Santa Cruz de la Cañada.

5. The *asesor-general* was the official legal adviser to the viceroy.

Account of Disorders, 1778

❖

F or an understanding of the character of society in
colonial New Mexico, interested readers can scarcely do
better than consult the many reports from the pens of the
Franciscan fathers who carefully observed and studied the
course of provincial affairs. One little known example is
Father Juan Agustín de Morfí's "Account of Disorders in
New Mexico, 1778."* Among other things, he criticizes
many of the habits and customs of the Spanish settlers,
comparing them unfavorably with the better disciplined
Pueblo Indians; condemns the injurious system of commerce
and barter practiced by New Mexican merchants; and urges
reform in the method of collecting compulsory church tithes.
In addition, Father Morfí discusses the social relations

*From a copy in the AGN, Historia, vol. 25.

*existing among the various ethnic groups—Spaniards,
Indians, Blacks, and mixed-bloods. He focuses special
attention upon the class of New Mexican people known as*
genízaros. *These were displaced Indians, usually members
of nomadic tribes, who as children had been captured or
ransomed by the Spaniards. Growing up in provincial
society, they lost most of their native heritage and became
Christians. But they lived in a kind of cultural and
economic limbo, accorded little status by Spanish citizens
and shunned by the Pueblos. Morfí, like other friars before
him, speaks here of the industry and courage of the
genízaros and recommends that the government provide
them with farmlands so that they can become self-sustaining
and an asset to New Mexico.*

*Only a few details are available concerning Juan
Agustín de Morfí's life. It is known that he was native to
the province of Asturias in northern Spain where many
Irish Catholics had settled, so it is supposed his surname is
a corruption of "Murphy." As a young man he immigrated
to Mexico City and there entered the Franciscan Order on
May 3, 1761. In time, Morfí developed an interest in the
missionary program of the northern provinces. As a result
of his travels there as well as his close study of the
documentary sources, he earned a reputation as an authority
on frontier matters. That led him to write extensively on the
subject and to serve as a consultant to the royal
government.*

*One of his shorter pieces of work is the "Account of
Disorders in New Mexico." Its contents and tone show him
to have been an intelligent and sensitive man, concerned
with the welfare and future of New Mexico and dedicated to
alleviating wrongs suffered by the Indians. He wrote in the
best tradition of that small group of Spaniards who, since*

128

*the days of earliest settlement in the New World, had posed
for official and public debate the nagging question, "What
measures should we take to ensure justice for the native
people?"*

*As a humanitarian, Father Morfí felt the obligation to
promote social reform. In "Disorders" he tried to point out
specific measures the royal government might take to
improve society and the economic lot of common citizens in
one of the remotest corners of the Spanish empire, the
province of New Mexico.*

THE ACCOUNT

I

1.   The Indians of New Mexico, even more than those
of Old [Mexico], disliked nomadic life from the time of
their pagan days before meeting the Spaniards. They
used to have and [still] have their pueblos in the best
of order, with one or more plazas in proportion to the
number of residents. They build their houses on streets
which are all arranged to empty into the main plaza that
ordinarily is round. Their buildings are of three, four,
and even seven stories without any means of going from
one to the other on the inside. Rather they climb from
the street to the [roof] of the first story, and from that
level to others, by ladders which are pulled up at night
to guard against surprise attack. And the people on the
roof tops can defend themselves, while enemies, roaming the streets, find no protection from arrows and stones
hurled from above.

By such means Don Juan de Oñate was able to

defend himself from the same natives when he was besieged in the Pueblo of San Juan de los Caballeros. Without this advantage he would have found himself overwhelmed by superior numbers.[1] In addition to this, the Indians surrounded their villages with earthworks, stockades, and ditches making them impregnable to enemies who are disorganized, ill-prepared, and fearful of the courageous residents. These precautions grew out of the hostilities they have always suffered at the hands of Apaches, Comanches, Navajos, and Utes by whom they are surrounded. With these [fortifications] and their natural bravery, they have from the beginning maintained law and order and instilled respect in all those who oppose them. The Pueblo of Sandía, which is smaller, for it is composed of thirty families, has never seen enemies inside its precincts. And here a handful of men, owing to an effective arrangement of houses, can bring fear to hundreds of warriors.

2.   This example teaches nothing to the Spaniards, who should be conducting themselves with more propriety and self-discipline than the Indians, [but who] are not ashamed to prove themselves ruder than the pagans. In all the kingdom [of New Mexico] there is not one town of Spaniards in good order. As if fleeing from the company of their brothers, they withdraw their habitations from one another, stringing them out in a line as fast as they can build them. So that, for example, the Villa of Alburquerque if reduced to a systematic arrangement would be a moderate size town and could offer abundant agricultural lands, pastures, and commons to its population. As things are, with its faulty arrange-

ment, it occupies today more than twelve leagues along
the banks of the river.[2]

3. From this disorder proceeds an infinite number of
others which are discovered by the most casual investigation. Since [the settlers] do not live under the scru-
tiny of the authorities, it is not easy for the latter to keep
track of the conduct of these subjects. They enjoy a kind
of independence that permits their larger crimes to go
unpunished because they are not detected. [They] are
deprived of the benefit of the Sacraments, a great many
dying without this aid because one lone minister who
must take care of one, two, three, or more towns at the
same time, cannot attend to those that are so far away.
And as a consequence they know less about religion
than the Indians themselves.

4. When it becomes necessary to muster arms for battle
or for pursuit of the enemy, our people take so long
getting together that the foe has plenty of time to carry
out its raid and escape.

5. Many live sunk in misery and without the means
of obtaining for themselves the basic necessities of life
because their practice of living dispersed, placing their
houses near the fields, not only encourages idleness but
also means the houses are prone to be raided, lacking
the protection of neighbors. So owing to this, they dare
not go out and work, or if they do, they become victims
of their own folly since the enemy, ever bold and swift,
sweeps through the communities with perfect liberty,
on account of their disorderly layout.

6.   As they live isolated with no one to observe them there are those who have no inhibitions about running around stark naked and as a result many have simply given up trying to obtain, through their own labor, the wherewithal to cover their nudity. Out of this, other moral disorders proceed which shock even the barbarous Indians, from whom such behavior cannot be hidden. As a result lewdness holds destructive sway here, more so than among animals. And even robbery is looked upon as a tolerable expedient that does not diminish one's reputation, so that blatant violence is the rule.

7.   Quite the contrary situation prevails among the Pueblo Indians. Their towns have a well-ordered economy under the eye of the local magistrate and minister. They attend Mass and partake of the Sacraments regularly. At the first sounding of the drum or ringing of the bell they all assemble to defend themselves or take the offensive. The closeness of their fields one to the other not only facilitates cultivation, but makes for greater security in case of a surprise attack. Cattle and horse herds of the pueblo are pastured in common and under a competent guard. And although on occasion they lose a few head, it is never as much or as often as the Spaniards. They are prone neither to thievery nor drunkenness. By moving their ladder a bit to the side, so that it is not in front of the door to the house, they show everyone that the owner is not at home, and no one dares violate this public trust. As a rule they freely harvest their crops and live in abundance.

It can be noted, then, that the only way the Spaniards are going to enjoy these benefits is by putting their towns in similar order. Yet when such is proposed, some

oppose abandoning their old houses, which is necessary, because it is to their own advantage and for the
good of the state.

II

8.   The second disorder that hinders the prosperity of
the kingdom [of New Mexico] has to do with the insid-
ious way in which trade is carried on, the evil juggling
of prices, and the illusory moneys which are used. All
these [practices] are directed toward taking advantage
of the innocent native people. The merchants abuse the
good name of Spaniards by doing the same things they
condemn Indians for, as if the latter are not due equal
treatment or even greater fairness in making a profit.
For after all, the Indians have recognized our authority
for two centuries, obeyed our laws, and firmly professed
the Christian religion.

9.   In order to make this point clearer, we must have
it understood that money doesn't even circulate in the
interior of the kingdom, and in the settlements around
El Paso scarcely at all. Business is conducted by barter
with the merchants trading things from Spain and Mexico, and receiving in return from the natives and [Span-
ish] citizens [of New Mexico] their own local products.
In El Paso such products are wheat, corns, beans, wine,
and liquor; and from the interior buckskin, buffalo hides,
blankets, embroidered clothes, stockings, and other things
made of wool and cotton and small quantities of pottery
and tanned sheepskins. These things constitute the
principal part of this defective and corrupt trade.

10.   Everywhere that the rule of law prevails and trading is done in good faith, exchanging and buying takes place not only when the harvests are gathered and the grain is stored in the granaries, but after a magistrate carefully sees to enforcement of laws which prohibit export until the needs of the province or kingdom that produced the crops are met. Thus, at least the inhabitants do not lack the necessary sustenance until the next planting. And whenever there is an abundance of civic spirit, public granaries have been established to which is consigned a certain portion of grain so as to keep the country from suffering in unproductive years and so that sowing the following year will not be prevented for lack of seed.

11.   Here [in New Mexico] just the opposite happens. Debts are incurred even before the seeds are planted and there are those who have sold their crops as much as six years in advance. Nothing is put aside, and a farmer who today eagerly takes up a hundred bushels of corn or wheat from the threshing floor, tomorrow must buy whatever else he needs to eat at four times the price of his own [goods] sold. Since he has no money and no additional harvest to pay for this purchase, he must mortgage his future in order to live. And if he has a family, however large, he must either see it suffer or commit the products of his labor many years in advance. He has no alternative. He sells for one rate and buys at another five times higher, and the disparity causes his debt to grow indefinitely.

12.   The initial debt is truly the tie that binds him to servitude from which he finds it impossible to escape

for the rest of his life. To fall into it, he doesn't have to be corrupt or a spendthrift. The cost of a marriage, a trip, a funeral, or some other out of the way expense no matter how small, is quite sufficient to lead him into this labyrinth of debt. A settler may need a hundred pesos for one of these things or for something similar. Since money does not circulate there, as I have said, to get what he needs, he has recourse to the merchant who will barter. But at what a markup! You now see where tyranny and fraud get their start.

13.   These merchants, not content with the monopoly by which they oppress the settlers, have invented illusory moneys [*monedas imaginarias*] to deceive them. These are of four kinds which are listed below according to their worth.

> Silver pesos valued at eight reales
> Inflated pesos [*de proyecto*] at six reales
> Old pesos at four reales
> Common pesos [*de la tierra*] at two reales

14.   This difference confuses the Indians and the settlers who think they make a profitable sale of their wares when they see that they are paid in pesos for a pint [*cuartillo*] of liquor, a string of chile, or a sack of corn, etc., without noticing that they are really paying the equivalent amount for a yard [*vara*] of ribbon that is priced by the *real*. The same goes for cheap cloth and other paltry goods. An example of each, that is, fair sales made by the merchants and the other sort, will show how they take advantage of and oppress their unfortunate customers. A length of ordinary cotton cloth which is called *judia* costs the merchant six pesos. A settler

needing to clothe himself buys it at a peso per yard, giving in place of pesos, pints of liquor. The piece, having 32 yards, costs him 32 pints of liquor. This miserable fellow then later goes to buy a pint of liquor at the house of the same merchant who sold him the cloth for common pesos [de la tierra]. But now the merchant tells him that in all honesty he must sell the liquor by the silver peso which results in the merchant getting in the long run 32 pesos for the original piece of cloth. From that, six pesos four reales are deducted for handling and losses of liquor, leaving him a profit of twenty-five pesos, four reales. The merchant makes collections at the end of the year [for goods bought on credit] and if the sale was made near harvest time, he will only have to carry the creditor for about two months.

15.   But as this amount is not received in cash, it is charged to the account of the buyer against his future harvest of corn; this is an example of the usual way sales are made. Corn by the sack [costal] is worth one old peso, (that is, four reales), and contains half a bushel [fanega] of grain. On account of that, twenty-five [silver?] pesos four reales buy twenty-five and a half bushels. These are then sold by the merchant to the presidial troops of San Elzeario, Principe, and Carrizal when they go to El Paso to purchase supplies of grain.[3] And ordinarily they pay the merchant twenty reales [per bushel] which means that he has made sixty-four pesos on that in the course of a year if the figuring begins with his original cost of six and a half pesos. On both the settler who sold him the grain and the soldier who bought it from him, he made a profit.

136

16.   If the cloth is not sold for liquor but immediately exchanged for grain, it has still another price. By the yard it is not worth a common peso (that is, two reales), but rather an old peso of four reales. This being the price of a half *fanega* of corn, thirty-two yards of cloth, thirty-two stockings, or sixteen bushels when sold each at twenty reales, bring forty [silver] pesos of eight reales on an original investment of six pesos in cloth.

17.   In the same manner the [merchants] buy from the poor Indians inside this province, they being the only ones who possess any surplus of sheep, buckskin, blankets, cloth, and pottery. Seed and grain, though abundant, do not figure regularly in this trade but play a part that I shall explain shortly. Abuse in business involving [Indians] is much greater, because of their nature and their confusion over the use of illusory moneys. Since they are not familiar with our customs, they are less able to discover fraud and to know the value of our wares. The conduct of one of the leading men of that kingdom [of New Mexico], named Don Francisco Trébol, can serve as proof of this.[4] This individual bought a Huacamaya [that is, a long-tailed parrot] for eight pesos and received four hundred ninety-two pesos in New Mexico for its feathers which is the only thing it produces. How did he do this? He tells whenever he's asked.

18.   It is not surprising that disorder grows out of this usury. A couple of cases will illustrate. There was a resident of El Paso, a certain Feliz, who is now a sergeant of the Presidio of Carrizal. He wanted to plant a few beans and not having any seed, he went to Don Manuel de la Torre to borrow some. The Don offered him what

137

he needed on condition that at the harvest he be given in return six bushels of beans or twenty-four sacks of corn. The present Father Vicar and Ecclesiastical Magistrate used to lend an *almud* [quarter bushel] on condition that he be given twelve in return. And it is currently the practice to give the Indians, especially during Holy Week, a jug of liquor obliging them to return a barrel at harvest time. This harmful practice destroys the last liberty of those persons who are already in a subservient position and adds to the burden which the use of illusory moneys places upon them. And they are seen to die in servitude owing hundreds of pesos, and without ever having a single day's proper nourishment or fit clothing for their bodies.

19.   Indeed, with this profitable business, [it seems] the merchants are getting rich, although that doesn't keep them out of harm's way. At the very least they ought to have something to show for what their wealth adds to the province. But the painful fact is that in spite of some large returns all are in miserable shape and none can show more than five hundred pesos in coin [*en reales*] on hand.[5] They are truly puppets of the Chihuahua merchants, from whom they get credit to run their own businesses and to whom they must repay with products of the country. The Chihuahuans, who know perfectly well the ins and outs of that business, overcharge for the goods they sell and knock down prices on what they buy. The result is that there is scarcely any margin with which the New Mexicans can pay freight and still support themselves even at a poverty level. Since they have no alternative, they are forced to accept the rules laid down in Chihuahua.

20.   As a first step, then, toward remedying this disorder means should be found for reducing the dependence of [New Mexico's] commerce upon that of Chihuahua. This will succeed in large measure if the principal goods traded or sold in the Villa [of Santa Fe] are manufactured within the province [of New Mexico] itself. This plan should be all the more useful, since it will be the easiest thing in the world to carry out. Wool is plentiful; cotton is so common that it is held in little regard. The fields and hills enchant one with the most beautiful and true colors I have ever seen, and there is an abundance of plants and minerals. Also, opportunity for industry is not lacking. Why then is it not developed? I will tell you later. Besides the articles of buckskin that are produced in the interior of the province, cotton blankets [*mantas*], sack cloth [*sayales*], and woolens [*paños*] are woven, and even a very good quality of plush [*tripe*], as Brigadier Don Pedro Fermín de Mendinueta testifies. I have seen coverlets [*colchas*] that in their variety of design and beauty of color are much better by comparison than those of Puebla and San Miguel El Grande which are so widely used in New Spain. I also saw a pillowcase made of very fine spun thread and with very delicate needle-work. And above all some cloaks [*manguillos*] of rabbit fur that delighted me. All this confirms the industriousness of the people and the abundance of raw materials. But not withstanding such opportunities, New Mexico cannot get a favorable trade going with neighboring provinces, nor for that matter can she avoid exploitation which, as we have seen, is bringing her to ruin.

21.   Since in this local industry there are no looms or

equipment to save time and labor and everything is done at the cost of much work, and without proper instruction, all articles take a long time to finish. So much effort is thus expended that goods cannot be sold at a reasonable price. Consequently, weaving will never be made a productive branch of trade. For example, woolens [*paños*] produced here are poorly regarded since they cannot be properly made, owing to a lack of fulling mills [*batanes*]. If workers were provided the help that they need, the unfavorable balance of trade would be corrected.

And is this so difficult? Hardly a day goes by that the Audiencia of Mexico, the Tribunal of the Acordada, and the Magistrate of the Liquor monopoly [*juez de chinquiritos*] do not sentence to prison for some small crime, Indians or common folk who are carpenters, loommakers, weavers, fullers, dyers, embroiderers, hatters, etc. Some of them could be sent here if the matter was handled properly, so as to include only those whose crimes do not indicate a spirit of total depravity and worthlessness. In this way the shortage of craftsmen could be remedied. The expense of sending them [here], I believe, would not be any greater than that needed to send them to Havana where many are incapacitated or even die from the change in climate or from the differences in working conditions that they are not used to. Here [in New Mexico] they would be happy and would make this fertile province more prosperous. There is a healthful climate, although cold in winter. The diseases to which the inhabitants are exposed are neither as many nor as deadly as those in Veracruz and other tropical areas. Outcasts could establish themselves to good advantage and with little trouble, if they mind their ways, and they would probably turn out to be very good settlers. Outside of El Paso [the center of wine and brandy production], there is no opportunity for them to fall victim to drunkenness, which usually was the thing that brought them to ruin in their hometowns.

22. It may be necessary to advance some moneys to allow for the assembling of materials, construction of looms and workshops, and for the maintenance of looms and workshops, and for the maintenance of masters and apprentices until such time as they can support themselves by their own labor.[6] But neither do I judge this to be very difficult if the following suggestions have some merit.

23. All the tithes in New Spain should be paid directly to the royal government, with no exceptions. The Church of Durango [for example] now receives the tithes of New Mexico, we can say unjustly, because it falls far short of providing these faithful members of the spiritual flock with the aid they deserve. The King is supporting through the Royal Treasury whatever priests there are in that kingdom [of New Mexico], all of which are and always have been members of the Franciscan Order. The only exception was a curate of El Paso called Las Caldas, whose parishioners after a short while fled to the hills and joined up with the Apaches in order to harrass us. Thus if the amount of tithes from both places, that is, from El Paso and from the upper province, are combined they come to the sum of three thousand eight hundred ninety-five pesos which if applied to the useful project mentioned above would in a few short years lead to prosperity and produce even greater Church revenues.

141

The Church would scarcely miss these tithes, since in the two previous years before this, it lost all the revenues of El Paso, which come to two thousand pesos, because of the lack of a lessee and collector. And if now they try to collect the overdue tithes they will end up destroying the communities, because the citizen could not pay what he owes even by selling all his lands. And in case [future] tithes [from El Paso] should be earmarked for this truly pious project [the development of industry], their collection and conversion [*venta*] could be given to the case of the Captain of the Presidio of San Elzeario while those from upper New Mexico could be handled by the Governor or his subordinate.

24.   But if this way seems inappropriate or impractical, the same tithing system offers still another means by which the Church itself can continue to collect an equal or even a larger sum than what would be necessary to fund the new industry project. I will explain. This information, in all its details, I acquired from knowledgeable persons, one of whom several times held the contract for collecting the tithes of the province.

25.   These tithes in their best years, among which is the current one, are farmed out for one thousand eight hundred ninety-five pesos. At present they are collected and administered efficiently under the new plan to benefit the promotion of industry, twenty thousand pesos could still be given to the Church, with enough left over to meet expenses of the labor project. The truth of this conclusion can be seen by reference to the amounts and values of what is presently collected, notwithstanding the Indian hostilities from which the province is suffer-

Plowing, New Mexican style. (From an early illustration in *Scribner's Magazine*)

ing. When these hostilities were less common, the value of the tithes was almost double the figure presented here.

1500 bushels [*fanegas*] of wheat at 12 reales per bushel amount to . . .	2250 pesos
3000 bushels of corn [*maiz*] at 12 reales . . .	4500 pesos
200 bushels of beans [*frijol*], chick peas [*garbanzo*], horse beans [*haba*], peas [*alverjón*], etc. at 3 pesos . . .	600 pesos
600 strings [*ristras*] of chile at 2 reales . . .	150 pesos

143

800 strings of onions at 2 reales . . .	200 pesos
250 *arrobas* [25 lb. measure] of wool at 2 pesos . . .	500 pesos
1000 chickens at 1 real each . . .	125 pesos
200 bunches [*manojos*] of *punchi* or wild tobacco, at 4 reales . . .	100 pesos
2500 head of sheep, half rams [*carnero*] and half ewes [*oveja*] at 1 peso each . . .	2500 pesos
100 head of cattle and horses [*ganado mayor*] at 3 pesos . . .	300 pesos
8 colts at 3 pesos . . .	24 pesos
12 hogs at 3 pesos . . .	36 pesos
Total	11,285 pesos

Taken together, then, the lump sum produced by the tithes [in upper New Mexico] comes to 11,285 pesos. If two thousand of this is given to the Church, and another two thousand is designated for freight and salaries [for transporting and collecting the tithes], some seven thousand two hundred eighty-five pesos would still be left for carrying out the development plan I have proposed. When this amount is added to the tax raised in a similar manner at El Paso, there should be enough to take care of all exigencies.

26. It is public knowledge that the current collector of tithes makes huge profits and engages in scandalous conduct as may be proved by what happened in the lease arrangements just completed. Don José Ortiz, *alcalde mayor* of the Villa of Santa Fe, made a bid to collect

the tithes, and being worried that Don Francisco Trébol and Don Clemente Gutiérrez might underbid him, he wrote to Trébol giving notice of his intent and trying to find out if they (who happened to be married to two sisters) were going to get together on their bid. To this, Trébol replied that the two of them were of a mind to go to the auction [*subasta*], but that they would withdraw immediately if Ortiz would give them two hundred pesos each and exempt them from paying tithes since their shares of the tax were the largest in the province. Ortiz refused their offer, and as a result Gutiérrez got the lease for the sum I have stated (one thousand eight hundred ninety-five pesos).

27. If my new industry project was established, by using the tithes or other taxes, there is no doubt that the province could develop important commercial relations with outposts in New California, Sonora, and Vizcaya. The New Mexicans, by selling their products for silver in these places, could then buy what they needed from Europe. And in bringing home large sums [of hard money] and putting them into circulation, they would destroy this contrived system of illusory moneys I described above, which is fed by avarice. This commerce would attract numerous people and would give a decent means of livelihood to many persons who today suffer involuntary idleness. With the number of consumers enlarged, the amount of land under cultivation would multiply and the revenue from tithes would experience a corresponding growth. The presidial troop could be doubled without increasing the amount now set aside for salaries because as the price of goods comes down [under the new system] soldiers' pay can be re-

145

duced accordingly without causing them any real loss. The soldiers themselves saw this happen when they made the switch from the old to the new *Reglamento*.[7] And finally, that Kingdom [of New Mexico] would become familiar with many valuable products which it now does not have owing to the lack of communication with our other frontier provinces. And among other things, perhaps cobalt and mercury will be found, for which possibility there exists solid and abundant evidence.

28.   In the meantime, I judge that it would be useful to abolish the illusory moneys and that the government monitor the conduct of the merchants to prevent the introduction of defective goods and to prevent them from cheating the Indians with regard to the quality and price of wares they are permitted to sell. Also, sale of cattle and seeds should be made at proper times in compliance with the ordinance of October 31, 1579, which provides that no Spaniard, Mestizo, Mulatto, or Negro anywhere in New Spain will be allowed to buy corn from the Indians in their houses, nor in any other such place, but that they should barter in the public markets and register the purchase the same day with the magistrates of the town where the trading, selling, etc., was done. If this ordinance is observed much of the disorder will be straightened out, the more so if it is extended to apply to the business dealings of all citizens. All trade that contributes to extravagances should be strictly forbidden since any display of luxury would be unseemly in view of the general state of misery that prevails [in New Mexico]. A colony inhabited by civilized and prudent people ought not to be suffering from want two

hundred years after its founding; but, a glance shows this condition persisting. To speak straightforwardly, the country is worse off than when it came under our control. Today the area in best condition is the rebellious province of Moqui [Hopi] which, being pagan and governed by no other laws than its ancient customs, conducts its own affairs quite ably. Not only other Indians but our own people as well have at times gone to the Hopi to secure livestock and seed, which [ironically] they acquired in the beginning from the Spaniards. Fathers Vélez and Martínez,[8] missionaries of Zuñi, in order to have chickens and milk to drink found it necessary to send and buy them from the Moqui people who carry on a wide trade in woven goods, livestock, and seeds with all the neighboring tribes and with those that occupy the banks of the Río Colorado down to its mouth on the Gulf of California, of which fact plenty of proof can be seen.

III

29. Although royal laws prohibit Spaniards, Mulattoes, Mestizos, and Negroes from living in Indian pueblos, they have never been obeyed with any strictness. And it is difficult to judge if the resulting intermingling of races is useful or harmful to the Indians themselves and to the State. It is undeniable that those Indians, in whose pueblos different races have gained admission, are more civilized, speak our language perfectly, embrace our customs, are more attentive to our religion, have greater respect for their property, and give better obedience to our magistrates. All these things are ad-

vantageous and should be pursued with great diligence, as in fact His Majesty has stated in repeated decrees to governors, bishops, priests, and missionaries. But all that aside, it is apparent that this admittance [of outsiders into the pueblos] and its tolerance in New Mexico has been one of the causes of the province's present retardation and of the Indians' ruin.[9]

30.   The Spaniards, under which name they include here also Mulattoes, Coyotes, Mestizos,[10] etc., even when they are offered good and fertile lands on which to settle prefer to move into the Indian pueblos. If they took up lands they would need to clear them, build houses, etc., which, without help of the government, would cost them a great deal of work and sweat. In the pueblos they find everything already done. With a little liquor, a few ribbons, some feathers, and other trifles of this kind, they entice the Indian who sells them his possessions, or they get him into debt. In the latter case, they turn the matter over to an *alcalde* and by using the law take away what the Indian has. Not content with this high-handedness, they shrewdly take advantage of the natural indifference of those miserable people to heap upon them new obligations, which they [the Indians] not being able to meet at the moment for lack of products, are obliged to pay off in work. In this way, an [Indian] man who yesterday lacked a square of cloth [*manta*] to cover himself, today is forced by necessity to enter domestic service much to his shame. And the poor Indian who had title to his lands by the same method becomes a virtual slave.

31.   Reduced to such an unhappy state, the Indian's only inclination is to abandon himself to vice in a bid

to render his misery less painful. His children are also the losers. And when the [native people] are harrassed by our magistrates, who either through some personal interest want to force them to work, or through zealousness in pursuing their notions of the public good seek to admonish them, they flee to the back country. Thus in a few years a good and productive family has been transformed into a blood-thirsty enemy, all the more to be feared because, being somewhat civilized, they know us better. The place they have abandoned suffers for lack of workers and everything is in a state of unrest.

32. In the town of El Paso, the Spaniards have by this means come into possession of the best lands and lots, and the Indians who were once owners of the town have found it necessary to leave it, lest they bring upon themselves the vices which we noted among the Spanish population. Thus, they are placed in the position of either perishing at the hands of enemy tribes or of entering into dangerous alliances with them. If a careful inquiry was made into the manner in which [Spanish] citizens have acquired their property, surely not one example could be found of land obtained legitimately.

33. This principal means of oppression, made worse by the haughtiness of the *castas* [mixed bloods], opens other opportunities for exploiting the native people. The Indians are supposed to have their own petty governor, but the Coyote or the Mulatto who lives among them and enjoys some power, works it so that either through an election or through selection by the local [Spanish] magistrate, he gets the job. And then, since he holds

the advantage in his hand, he does what he pleases. He keeps in mind, though, that it was the magistrate who allowed him the job and it is the Protector who tolerates him in it.[11] But even after paying them off, he still winds up with no small share for himself. This kind of man is given to committing the worst sort of injustices and cruelties. The cause lies with his evil mind which is a product of his inferior birth and lack of any education. As a consequence, this rascal's treatment of the Indians is guided by hatred and arrogance. And this abuse has become so widespread, that it frequently can be found in other provinces. An example can be seen at present in the town of Nombre de Dios [Nueva Vizcaya] whose Indians made complaints to the government secretary about such conditions. And if a separate accounting were made of all the cases of injustice that exist here [in New Mexico], this list would be interminable.

34. Having considered all this, it must be noted that if we could get the Spaniards to improve their treatment of the Indians, observe the royal laws (whose present neglect keeps the two peoples at loggerheads), and put an end to the aforementioned oppression, this combination would produce the most beneficial results imaginable. And I judge this to be self-evident and quite easy to put into practice.

35. All outsiders in an Indian pueblo should be expelled, as the law requires. And they should be assigned a site for a new settlement in the vicinity of the pueblo so that the two populations can continue to intermingle, although within set limits, to prevent entanglements over land.

150

36.   Spaniards and mixed-bloods should be prohibited from acquiring any property within the Indian pueblos unless it is by inheritance through a mixed marriage. If this was in effect, the desire of non-Indians to acquire property would make them more amenable to have Indians as sons-in-law. Knowing that such alliances would be beneficial, they would encourage them. Then they would not look on these marriages with such scorn. At present a Mulatto considers himself disgraced if his daughter chooses an Indian for a husband. Such a case arose at [the Presidio of San Juan Bautista del] Río Grande, where a Mulatto, discovering that his daughter wished to marry an Indian of the Mission of San Bernardo, brought suit asking that the Indian be punished for his audacity and the missionary be reprimanded for not having prevented the entire affair.[12]

37.   It should be a requirement that neither those who by marriage are admitted to the pueblos, nor their children can hold public office there, as long as the majority of the residents remain pure Indians. This would forestall unfavorable consequences arising from any natural antipathy that might exist between the Indians and mixed-bloods.

38.   With respect to the lands of the Indians, there should be faithful observance of what has been ordered by the law inserted in the Ordinance of December 17, 1603, which provides: "That whenever the Indians must sell their lands for any reason, unless their worth be under thirty pesos, His Majesty directs that a public notice of thirty days be given so that they can be auctioned to the highest bidder. During the thirty day period, first

and foremost there must be held the necessary proceedings and investigations to study the Indians' land, inherited from their parents, and to determine that they have other lands of value remaining, sufficient for working and providing a living. And this being done and the public notice given, which is required before the auction, the proceedings should be brought before Your Excellency in order to prove that the sale is desirable.[13] All this should be done in the proper manner, for if it is conducted in any other way, the sale will be null and void." There is no doubt that if this law and ordinance were observed throughout America, the people would be much better off.

39. The proximity of the pueblo to [the non-Indian town], the ease with which marriages could be arranged, and the daily conduct of trade would bring to the Indians the aforementioned benefits. At the same time, the separation of houses and fields, observance of the laws, which prohibit sale of strong liquors to Indians, and the diligence of magistrates and missionaries could keep them from indulging in vice. Without such protection [the Indians] through the above-mentioned contact and trade, would find themselves expelled from their pueblos and condemend to servitude.

IV

40. To this point, we have seen how poorly the royal laws are observed in New Mexico, especially those that are aimed at the welfare and protection of the Indians. But now we will look at another scandal and [see] that

the worst harm which these unhappy people suffer comes at the hands of those very persons who ought to be working continuously to provide them protection. Those subjects [that is, government officials] to whom the King has delegated a part of his authority and has entrusted his moral responsibility are the first in the rush to devour the Indians, and though they bleed them dry, they still are not satisfied. I'm speaking here of the *alcaldes mayores*. There [in New Mexico], these [persons] are a sorry lot without education or proper breeding, mostly mixed-bloods. And if there chance to be a Spaniard among them, or one or another European, he was brought in under the sponsorship of the missionaries, or he came in the service of some governor. These [men], then, who are charged with the administration of justice, manage, as they say, to take advantage of their term to exploit the Indians. To aid them, lieutenants [*teniente alcaldes*] are named who are capable of assisting in their designs. These *alcaldes* generally live outside their jurisdictions, and each pueblo is required to donate rations and carry them to their place of residence. This consists of a sheep per week, plus butter, beans, and tortillas for each one. And if the *alcalde* goes away for a time, he gets all the donations in a lump when he returns. Such is the usual practice. Besides this, the Indians have to perform personal service. This is beyond the required domestic service in the *alcaldes'* houses. The Indians are forced to plant and cultivate their lands, walking from the pueblos the whole day and sometimes much more with farm implements on their shoulders in order to get from their villages to the fields of the *alcaldes*. If there is much work, as in the case of Trébol, who annually raises two hundred bushels [*fanegas*] of wheat and about three hundred of corn, often the entire pueblo is kept busy the greater part of the year. In January they prepare the land, in February they begin cultivating, and by October they finish up. In the interval all the work pertaining to raising corn is done. The remaining months when the men are not farming, the women go to work grinding at the *metates*. This takes all of October and November. Some idea of their work load can be gained by reference to the activities of Trébol, who, for one of his trips to Chihuahua, made the Indian women grind eighteen bushels of wheat, many more of corn, and eighty strings of chile.[14]

41.   The *alcaldes* are the only ones who trade with the Indians, from whom they get seeds and brood stock by exchanging the most useless trifles, as we have seen in the case of Trébol's parrot. By means of this trade, of the enforced donations, and the annual toil with which they burden the Indians, the *alcaldes* are making themselves masters of all the livestock in the province. The Indians shear, wash, and sort the wool, and the *alcaldes*, still not content with this, distribute it and assign them the added task of weaving and oblige them to return finished cloth [*mantas*]. Still there's more. The Indians have to deliver everything on their mules, where and when the *alcaldes* wish it. And if on the road, they lose, break, or damage something, it is charged against the Indian responsible. In spite of performing all this work and service, neither they, nor their daughters, nor their wives, are given recompense even for their daily expenses. If the *alcalde* has the contract for tithe collection, as has happened with Trébol, and usually happens with Clemente Gutiérrez, all year the poor Indians have to

work as mule packers and furnish any animals which the *alcalde* may be short, with the same lack of remuneration. One is appalled at the disregard for the royal laws which provide that, "under no circumstances may *alcaldes* demand or receive anything from the Indians, nor may they engage in trade or buy seeds or livestock, even under the pretext that these are necessary for food, and not even Indians who are lawbreakers can be condemned to perform personal service for the benefit of some private person." But one is horrified to the soul to see what lengths tyranny is carried by these who betray the good name of Spaniards and exploit the Indians.

42.   Beyond the grinding service which large groups of Indian women perform when they go to the *alcalde's* house, they also year around provide daily labor required in his kitchen and at his *metates*. These women are chosen arbitrarily by the *alcaldes,* and even when by some good fortune they are paid, never has a group of women gone away without suffering personal outrage, a fact that causes their fathers and husbands perpetual sorrow. If the Indians one year have enough means to buy their liberty and thus preserve their honor, the next year they lack it. And for this reason, there is scarcely a single soul who escapes abuse.

43.   And what benefits do the Indians receive from these *alcaldes?* It is well known that they never go to the pueblos under their jurisdiction except when they are out to make the levies and to collect the debts that have piled up. And there is no evidence that on such occasions these gentlemen perform any service that is useful to

155

the Indians. The list of those who are most infamous and tyrannical is public knowledge: Clemente Gutiérrez, Francisco Trébol, Baltasar Baca, Pedro Pino, Nerio Montoya, Manuel Vigil, and José Miguel de la Peña, or better said, everyone who has ever served in those offices (with very few exceptions). Each one [at the beginning of his term] finds the evil practices so firmly established, he doesn't want to miss the chance of taking advantage of them. Many other abuses exist with regard to this matter, as anyone who delves into it will find out.

44.   This situation with the *alcaldes*, which is the source of the greatest harm, also happens to be the problem needing the least attention to see it remedied. For nothing more is necessary than the observance of the royal laws that govern the matter and the stern punishment of offenders, with the penalties that the laws themselves provide.

V

45.   In all the Spanish towns of New Mexico there exists a class of Indians called *genízaros*. These are made up of captive Comanches, Apaches, etc., who were taken as youngsters and raised among us, and who have married in the province. Since they are the offspring of enemy tribes, the natives of this province, who bear long grudges, never admit them to their pueblos. Thus [the *genízaros*] are forced to live among the Spaniards, without lands, or other means to subsist except by the bow and arrow which serves them when they go into the back country

to hunt deer for food. They are fine soldiers, very warlike, and most formidable against our enemies. They desire sites for villages but fail to obtain any, either because no one wants to provide them or because most lands have been occupied through the making of excessive and fraudulent grants [*donaciones*] to Spaniards. Thus, there are no lands that can conveniently be given. Expecting the *genízaros* to work for daily wages is folly because of the abuses they have experienced, especially from the *alcaldes mayores*, when they have tried in the past. These are men, who, granted the rights of citizens, would prove very useful in times of war. But now, on account of their poverty, which leaves them afoot and without arms, they have little chance to serve. They bewail their neglect and they live like animals.

46.   In two places, Belén and Tomé, some sixty families of *genízaros* have congregated. They have petitioned for formal community rights and, hoping to get them, they sent representatives [south] with the current trade caravan. The chief spokesman among these went on to Durango at the behest of Lieutenant Colonel Don Juan Bautista de Anza.

47.   By way of establishing that their request is reasonable, it should be noted that what they are seeking is the site called El Sabinal. This is a dangerous frontier point which faces the Ladrón Mountains, a refuge of our enemies [the Apaches]. This place is very well suited for the formation of a town, and its lands are so fertile that the [Spanish] citizens of Belén sought permission from Brigadier Don Pedro Fermín de Mendinueta to start farming there. Since he knew the site was suitable

for a new and large settlement, he granted the request for the present, but on condition that the men leave their families in Belén, taking care not to depopulate that town and not to place their women and children in such a dangerous location [as El Sabinal]. But those Spaniards, in the habit of disregarding official orders, moved some of their families anyway and built themselves some houses in the same disorderly and careless manner as in Belén. That is to say, their huts are distant from each other a quarter of a league or more. The result is that instead of [this new outpost] restraining [hostile] Indians, it merely provides them opportunity for satisfying their cruelty and greed.

48. It appears, therefore, that it would be best to confine the Spaniards to the town of Belén and grant the site [of El Sabinal] to these *genízaros*. When they construct a new pueblo in the same orderly style as the [Pueblo] Indians, it would be like a fort. When you add to that, the bravery of the residents, dedicated to the preservation of their property and families, you have a defensive shield protecting the town of Belén. And the immediate vicinity would be closed to the forays of Comanches, who are greatly feared. [The *genízaros*] could make an easy and honest living. They would respond promptly to calls for campaign duty, and at no cost to the Royal Treasury. And finally there would be one more town added to the realm.

49. In the same way, the many remaining families of *genízaros*, who roam about the province, ought to be congregated and have appropriate sites provided for them. Thus, they could get established, independent of

the Spaniards and have officials chosen from among themselves. In doing this, they should be encouraged, assisted, and honored with the same privileges and exemptions enjoyed by other Indians [that is, the Pueblos]. For they deserve all this on account of their loyalty and the continuous services they have rendered on military campaigns.

NOTES TO ACCOUNT OF DISORDERS IN NEW MEXICO

1. This refers to an incident described by Oñate's subordinate, Gaspar Pérez de Villagrá, in his *Historia de Nuevo Mexico*, first published in Spain in 1610. For a recent translation see the one made by Gilberto Espinosa, *History of New Mexico* (Los Angeles, 1933). This work was widely distributed in New Spain during colonial times and Father Morfí obviously had access to it.

2. This was a common complaint made by both religious and civil officials throughout the colonial period. For example, Bishop Pedro Tamarón visiting the capital in 1760 remarked that, "Santa Fe is a very open place; the houses are far apart; and therefore it does not have the least defense." Eleanor B. Adams, ed., *Bishop Tamarón's Visitation of New Mexico, 1760*, Historical Society of New Mexico, Publications in History, XV (1954), p. 47. The tendency of the Spanish New Mexicans to disperse their homes and villages is described fully in Marc Simmons, "Settlement Patterns and Village Plans in Colonial New Mexico," *Journal of the West*, VIII (1969), p. 7–21.

3. These three presidios were in the jurisdiction of Nueva Vizcaya.

4. On this and several subsequent occasions in his report, Father Morfí singles out Francisco Trébol Navarro for criticism. Nothing is known of the man's origin and Fray Angélico Chávez, *Origins of New Mexico Families* (Santa Fe, 1954), p. 296, suggests he came to New Mexico sometime after the mid-eighteenth century. He was married by the missionary of Isleta in 1765, and then or later owned a ranch at nearby Pajarito. In 1778 Trébol was *alcalde mayor* and

capitán of militia at Albuquerque when retiring Governor Mendi-nueta appointed him acting-governor of New Mexico to serve until the arrival of Juan Bautista de Anza. Bancroft, *History of Arizona and New Mexico,* p. 264.

5. This statement appears to contradict Morfí's earlier assertion that no hard money circulated in New Mexico. Other writers of the day made a similar claim, yet we know that a certain amount of coin, for military expenditures, for example, found its way into the próvince.

6. In 1789 the colonial government assembled documents concerning the possibility of establishing a textile factory or workshop in Santa Fe. Therein, the "late" Father Morfí was quoted as favoring such a project. Expediente sobre establecimiento de un obraje en la Villa de Santa Fe de N. Mexico. A.G.N., Mexico, Provincias Internas, vol. 161.

7. It is not clear here whether Morfí is referring to the Reglamento de Presidios of 1772 or to new regulations on coinage issued by Charles III in the same year.

8. The two priests mentioned as serving at Zuñi were Fray Silvestre Vélez de Escalante and Fray Damián Martínez.

9. The policy that Spaniards and Indians should live apart was one adopted early by the royal government. It was intended, not to discriminate against the Indians, but to protect them from exploitation. On the laws pertaining to racial separation see Magnus Mörner, *Race Mixture in the History of Latin America* (Boston, 1967), pp. 45–48.

10. There is no general agreement among scholars on the meaning of the terms *coyote* and *mestizo* as used in colonial New Mexico. One view holds that *coyote* referred to a mixture of Spaniard and New Mexican Indian (either Pueblo or nomad) and *mestizo* to the offspring of Spaniard and Mexican Indian, such as Aztec or Tlax-calan. However, Fray Angélico Chávez suggests that a *coyote* was the child of a European-born father and a New Mexican mother, whether Spanish or Indian. And he postulates that a *mestizo* in this province was the product of a Spanish New Mexican father and an Indian mother, Pueblo or nomad. See "José Gonzales, Genízaro Governor," *New Mexico Historical Review,* XXX (1955), pp. 192–93. Obviously more research is needed if these and other colonial ethnic terms used in New Mexico are to be defined with any precision.

11. The *protector partidario* was the Indians' public defender nominated by the provincial governor. For a discussion of his functions see Marc Simmons, *Spanish Government in New Mexico* (Albuquerque, 1968), pp. 189–91.

12. This presidio was located at the present village of Guerrero, Coahuila, near the Río Grande and thirty-five miles southeast of modern Eagle Pass, Texas. Mission San Bernardo, begun in the 1760s, stood a short distance north of the presidio.

13. "Your Excellency" in this case probably referred to the Viceroy of New Spain.

14. It was a deliberate royal policy to keep the salary of petty civil officers small, or, as in the case of the *alcaldes mayores* in New Mexico, dispense with salaries altogether. Such officials were allowed to pocket small fines imposed for violations of the law, but these never amounted to more than a token sum. The results of this situation proved disastrous since under-rewarded bureaucrats manipulated their offices for personal profit and seized the many opportunities open to them for cheating the Indians.

Report of Governor Chacón, 1803

❖

N *ear the end of the colonial period, in 1803, New Mexico Governor Fernando de Chacón prepared a concise but highly useful report on the state of the provincial economy.* On February 14 of that year, his immediate superior in Chihuahua, Commandant General Nemesio Salcedo, had written a letter directing Chacón to assemble information on New Mexico's agriculture, industry, manual arts, and trade and forward it to the* consulado, *or merchant guild, of the Mexican port city of Veracruz. That guild, it seems, had the duty of compiling data from throughout the Viceroyalty of New Spain so that it could be used in shaping future economic reform.*

*Report of Governor Fernando de Chacón, Santa Fe, 28 August 1803, doc. no. 2, 1670a, Spanish Archives of New Mexico, State Records Center and Archives, Santa Fe.

As near as can be determined, Governor Chacón based his report on personal observation, on information supplied by associates, and perhaps on records preserved in the Santa Fe archive. The document furnishes a convenient overview of conditions in New Mexico, as he saw them. It was completed and promptly dispatched to the consulado at Veracruz in late August.

Fernando de Chacón served an eleven-year tenure (1794–1805) as chief executive at Santa Fe. He was one in a string of able and forceful governors who managed New Mexico's affairs in this period. His economic report, translated below, contains astute comments on provincial life and offers pointed suggestions for improving those spheres of public and private endeavor that were unquestionably retarded. Some of the governor's words that show him impatient with the local people and their customs contain an echo of similar complaints made by several of his predecessors. Withal, the content of Chacón's report confirms that he was dedicated to amelioration of the economic ills besetting New Mexico.

THE REPORT

By virtue of what was called for by the Señor Commandant General of the Internal Provinces, Don Nemesio Salcedo, in an official letter of May 2 which [came] as a result of His Majesty's Royal Order of June 21, 1802, directing the following: that the Tribunal of the Consulado of Veracruz be provided with the information it requests and needs regarding agriculture, industry, arts, and commerce of the various territories of this kingdom, in this case as pertains to the province of New Mexico, which presently is in my charge, the assignment is carried out in conformity with what I know about such matters.

The Province of New Mexico is the most northerly of all the Provincias Internas. It enjoys a very healthful climate with high mountains in the northern part and in the other directions. Also there are great open spaces, particularly to the east where the plains are expansive. Its sky is clear; the air pure and very cold in winter. Its fine and healthful waters that bathe it [come from] springs, some of them thermal, and different rivers among which the most important is the one called the Rio del Norte. Though it passes seventy leagues through the province, it does not carry much water upon crossing it as is believed. [New Mexico's] extent from north to south is sixty-seven leagues and from east to west eighty, leaving apart the Jurisdiction of El Paso which is separated from the interior of the province by a distance of ninety leagues. The major part of the population is located along the Rio del Norte, on one bank or the other, with the capital at the villa of Santa Fe situated in the center upon a little stream of no consequence and distant three leagues from the aforementioned Rio del Norte.

The number of souls of both sexes, including the Jurisdiction of El Paso del Norte, comes to, a little more or less, thirty-five thousand seven-hundred and fifty-one persons.

Agriculture in said Province does not appear in the best state owing to a lack of know-how. Nevertheless, the most common grains are sown, like wheat, corn and barley, and all kinds of vegetables in limited quantity, there being no practical way to export them to other provinces because of the great distances intervening between all of them. As a result the majority of its inhabitants are little dedicated to farming, in particular the Spaniards and *castas* who content themselves with sowing and cultivating only what is necessary for their sustenance. [Living] by luck through the scarce years, like the current one, they experience great need which is met by resort to wild plants, roots, milk, beef and mutton. As a consequence the development of these last two pursuits [that is, cattle and sheep raising] has not been more rapid. On the contrary the Pueblo Indians who compose a third of the population, develop large fields that are cultivated in common, so that they can take care of widows, orphans, the sick, the unemployed and those who are absent. By doing this and by reserving [part of] the harvest from one year to the next, they never feel the effects of hunger. Furthermore, they apply themselves to the cultivation of gardens, orchards and vineyards. In the same manner they are the ones best able to bring in a planting of cotton with which they make cloth (*mantas*) for their own use.

Tobacco is cultivated through careful handling by all the citizenry in general. But in spite of the effort required, one can profit nicely. The major part of the clergy smokes it or dips it as snuff.

In view of what has been said, it would be well if the superior authorities would vouchsafe to send to this Province, it being an easy matter and of small cost, books on agriculture illustrating for the residents everything pertaining to planting; methods of controlling insects which greatly reduce the harvests; the method of planting trees and grafting; the treatment of different illnesses affecting cattle, sheep and horses; knowledge of the use of herbs; or other innumerable things, etc., all of which they have here only the remotest idea.

Although the Province possesses sufficient oxen for farming, what is most in abundance is sheep. Without counting what is consumed locally, there is exported to [Nueva] Vizcaya and the lesser [frontier] presidios from one year to the next from twenty-five to twenty-six thousand head of sheep. Of swine there exists no great number because the natives of this country are more accustomed to the use of fat from beef than from hogs, and there is no one dedicated to the manufacture of soap. The raising of horses and mules is little encouraged because of the continual raids by the enemy [Indians]. But annually more than 600 animals of each kind are brought in from Sonora and Vizcaya, not counting the herds of mustangs (*mesteñada*), which the citizenry are in the habit of hunting whenever they go out on the frontier.

At different points in the Province have been found deposits of minerals such as silver, lead, tin, and copper. The last is very abundant and seems to be of a rich grade. There is also another copper, less fine, that is blue and green, which can serve as paint, but it is not utilized. For the smelting of said metals, there is also much coal of the best quality, which I believe is not common in all of New Spain. And in case silver should ever be smelted by means of the mercury process, there will be found nearby copious salt deposits, that being one of the principal ingredients of said operation. Of alum, jet, and ochre, which are easily found in great abundance, no use is made on account of there being no one to identify and take possession of it. Neither [do they exploit] soapstone which is useful in extracting the grease from woolen

A Spanish ox cart plods toward the Ortiz (in colonial times called the Placer or Gold) and Sandia mountains. (A drawing by R. H. Kern in the late 1840s)

cloth in fulling mills. Mica or gypsum (*yeso*) occurs, of fine quality and so transparent that in all the Province it covers windows in place of glass panes. It is also used to whitewash walls. The only use made of limestone is in the preparation of *nixtamal* (corn dough) through the hulling of corn kernels [by soaking in lime water]. The use of cement is not known to these people in the raising of their buildings, construction being performed with mud [mortar] and unfired adobe bricks.

With regard to arts and crafts it can be properly said that they do not exist in this Province because of the unavailability in those areas of apprenticeships, official examinations for the office of master, organized guilds and all the rest that is customary everywhere else. But

167

by necessity and the natural ingenuity of these people, some trades are practiced, for example, those of wool weaver, shoemaker, carpenter, tailor, blacksmith, and mason, in all of which they are skilled. The first [that is, weavers] produce, on narrow loom combs, cloth for coats, serge, blankets, serapes, baize, sackcloth, and carpeting, which cloths they dye with indigo and brazilwood imported from outside, urine [as a mordant], and herbs that they are familiar with. From cotton they make a kind of cloth (*manta*) of twisted cord more closely woven and stronger than that from Puebla. Textiles for altar cloths and stockings [are also made]. Although the present government has furnished the said wool weavers with design plans for fulling devices and presses, it has not been practical to build either of these machines, the excuse being they cannot stand the cost. And for the same reason, or on account of laziness, carpenters will not use the two-man frame pit saw (*sierra bracera*), and as a result there is much wasting of wood.

Besides wool, of which there is an unlimited abundance in the Province, skins of rabbit, of several kinds of squirrel, and of beaver, for making hats, are also common. But this trade is not practiced because ability and inclination are lacking, and the same is true for the trades of tanner, leather dresser, saddler and others which make use of all kinds of pelts and hides. These last are found in great numbers and of many kinds, to wit: elk, common deer, bucks, wild sheep, buffalo, bear, mountain lion, wolf, fox, and coyote.

The abundance of copper, which can be extracted with little work, offers opportunities for the occupation of coppersmith, if there were artisans of this class and someone who knew how to smelt said metal. The trade of potter which produces ordinary wares as well as jars, crocks, cooking pots, flat bowls, etc., is pursued by the Pueblo Indians who make everything patiently by hand, instead of using a wheel, which is their way. Afterwards they fire it with manure and without using anything for glaze because they are not familiar with this material.

Commerce with the outside which this Province undertakes once each year with Sonora, Vizcaya, and Coahuila consists in oxen, sheep, woolen textiles, and some raw cotton, hides, piñons, which being much esteemed for their quality are easily sold, and wines that until now have only been produced in the Jurisdiction of El Paso del Norte. However, in the interior of the Province they are propagating the planting of vineyards and the production of some wine and brandy. Still it will be quite some time before the demand will be such that there is anything like common consumption. We are able to reckon the value of all the aforesaid at 140,000 pesos [annually].

The products mentioned are carried out by mule trains accompanied by 500 men, some of whom are merchants and others packers. They depart in the month of November with a military escort. They remain together as far as the town of El Paso, at which point they divide. About a third of them head for Sonora, Coahuila, and several of the lesser presidios. The remainder continue to Vizcaya with some of them stretching the journey on to the capital of Durango and its environs. Those stopping in the villa of Chihuahua conduct business to provision themselves with necessities.

The products brought back consist of horses, mules, linen goods, cotton textiles of all kinds, without excluding first and second grade cloths and [those from] Querétaro, baize, serge, scarlet, *chalonas,* silk cloths with both twisted and loose [threads], chocolate, sugar loaves, soap, rice, iron in merchant bars and plate, general hardware, spices, hats, leather goods of all sorts, pelts, tanned leather, paper, drugs, and some money, all of which assortment not only is sufficient to meet the expectations of the Province, but many of the aforementioned products are left over from one year to the next.

The internal commerce [of New Mexico] is in the hands of twelve or fourteen [local] merchants who are neither properly licensed nor well versed in business matters. Of these, only two or three are operating with their own capital. Among the rest everything they handle or bring into the Province is on credit. And they distribute and sell in the same way from one year to the next, with the result that only once a year do they get money in hand. And there are many losses and arrears in the collection of credit accounts, since these are regularly extended to the poorest people and at excessive rates. All of this is exacerbated by the lack of money in circulation which has begun to be experienced over the last three years. The situation still affects many [people] and in particular the Indians who do not have much use for it [that is, money] anyway.

The rest of the citizenry are so many petty merchants who are continuously dealing and bartering with whatever products they have at hand. Territorial magistrates are forced to mediate these exchanges [which are attended by] malicious and deceitful behavior and bad faith. Only does formality prevail in the trading carried on with the nomad Indians (*Naciones gentiles*), that being a give-and-take business conducted in sign language.

The products traded by the Spaniards to said nomad Indians are horses, saddlebags, *anqueras* (leather skirt covering the horse's rump), bits, hatchets, war axes, lances, knives, scissors, scarlet cloth, serapes, cloaks, woolens, indigo, vermilion, mirrors, [illegible interlinear word], loaf sugar, native tobacco, corn in flour and on the ear, bread, and green or dried fruit. In exchange, the nomads give Indian captives of both sexes, mules, moccasins, colts, mustangs, all kinds of hides and buffalo meat. The result is that the balance of the trade between the two parties always comes out in favor of the Spaniards.

The common woods in this Province are cottonwood, oak, and pine, the last occurring in great abundance. Its extraction by means of rafts on the Rio del Norte is not difficult. But these people do not know of any place or destination where they can take it and by which they can profit. For that reason no one is engaged in this branch of industry.

The description of New Mexico that I have given to this point, although succinct owing to the fact that my instructions did not require me to delve deeper and to speak authoritatively about all matters, perhaps will suffice to give a small idea [of the fact] that the Province is not really so poor as is [generally] supposed, and that its [seemingly] natural decadence and backwardness is traceable to the lack of development and want of formal knowledge in agriculture, commerce, and the manual arts. Through the charity of the King, [New Mexico] enjoys a ten year exemption from paying the sales tax (*alcabala*) with the result that not only has it failed to contribute anything to the Royal Treasury since the time of the Reconquest, but it annually costs His Majesty from 54 to 55 thousand pesos in stipends for the missionaries, salaries of the governor and lieutenant-governor, soldiers' pay, and annuities for the allied Indian nations.

Another clear proof that the Province is not poor can be found in the excessive display of luxuries, as compared to the rest of the Internal Provinces. They [the New Mexicans] don't experience famines, even though they get no relief aid from elsewhere, because they are able to augment their diet with an abundance of meat in those years when there is scarcity of grains and vegetables. One sees [here] no nakedness or begging. But in spite of the opulence, [the Province] will continue to decay by necessity, if you overload it with taxes before extending assistance to those [aforementioned] areas where it is deficient, including the discovery and processing of its metals.

Santa Fe, New Mexico
28th August of 1803

Selected Readings

⟡

The literature on Hispanic New Mexico, while not as volu-
minous as that on the Indians, is still astonishingly plentiful
and varied. It ranges from translated accounts of explorers,
settlers, missionaries, soldiers, and government officials
through modern compilations of folk literature and customs.
The listing given here incorporates titles that should have the
broadest appeal for the general reader and that also are both
recent and accessible.

Among the numerous historical and cultural surveys of
the area, the following can be highly recommended: Nancie
L. González, *The Spanish-Americans of New Mexico, A Heritage
of Pride* (Albuquerque: University of New Mexico Press, 1967);
Arthur L. Campa, *Hispanic Culture in the Southwest* (Norman:
University of Oklahoma Press, 1979); Aurelio M. Espinosa,
The Folklore of Spain in the American Southwest (Norman: University of Oklahoma Press, 1985); Nancy Hunter Warren, *Villages of Hispanic New Mexico* (Santa Fe: School of American

Research Press, 1987); Christine Mather, ed., *Colonial Frontiers: Art and Life in Spanish New Mexico* (Santa Fe: Ancient City Press, 1983).

Two outstanding overviews of material culture are: Marta Weigle, ed., *Hispanic Arts and Ethnohistory in the Southwest* (Santa Fe: Ancient City Press, 1983); and E. Boyd, *Popular Arts of Spanish New Mexico* (Santa Fe: Museum of New Mexico Press, 1974). The best introductory survey of the subject is still Roland F. Dickey, *New Mexico Village Arts* (reprint ed., 1990; Albuquerque: University of New Mexico Press, 1949).

Books on Hispanic culture that focus upon specialized topics abound. Some of the best include: Charles L. Briggs, *The Wood Carvers of Córdova, New Mexico* (Knoxville: University of Tennessee Press, 1980); José E. Espinosa, *Saints in the Valley* (Albuquerque: University of New Mexico Press, 1960); Ronald L. Grimes, *Symbol and Conquest: Public Ritual and Drama in Santa Fe, New Mexico* (Ithaca, NY: Cornell University Press, 1976); Bainbridge Bunting, *Early Architecture in New Mexico* (Albuquerque: University of New Mexico Press, 1976); John Donald Robb, *Hispanic Folk Music of New Mexico and the Southwest* (Norman: University of Oklahoma Press, 1980); Flavia Waters Champe, *The Matachines Dance of the Upper Rio Grande* (Lincoln: University of Nebraska Press, 1983); Paul Kutsche and John R. Van Ness, *Cañones: Values, Crises, and Survival in a Northern New Mexico Village* (Albuquerque: University of New Mexico Press, 1981); and Victor Westphall, *Mercedes Reales, Hispanic Land Grants of the Upper Rio Grande Region* (Albuquerque: University of New Mexico Press, 1983).

Finally, in the area of folklife and customs, the following titles can be mentioned: Cleofas M. Jaramillo, *Shadows of the Past* (Santa Fe: Ancient City Press, n.d.); Marc Simmons, *Witchcraft in the Southwest, Spanish and Indian Supernaturalism on the Rio Grande* (Lincoln: University of Nebraska Press, 1980); Lorin W. Brown, *Hispano Folklife of New Mexico* (Albuquerque: University of New Mexico Press, 1978); and Marta Weigle, *Brothers of Light, Brothers of Blood: The Penitentes of the Southwest* (Santa Fe: Ancient City Press, 1989).

Index